HEARING THE MERMAID'S SONG

Hearing the Mermaid's Song

The Umbanda Religion in Rio de Janeiro

LINDSAY HALE

UNIVERSITY OF NEW MEXICO PRESS

ALBUQUERQUE

LIBRARY OF CONGRESS CATALOGING-IN-PUBLICATION DATA

Hale, Lindsay.
Hearing the mermaid's song :
the Umbanda religion in Rio de Janeiro / Lindsay Hale.
p. cm.
Includes bibliographical references and index.
ISBN 978-0-8263-4733-6 (pbk. : alk. paper)
1. Umbanda (Cult)—Brazil—Rio de Janeiro.
2. Spirit possession—Brazil—Rio de Janeiro.
3. Rio de Janeiro (Brazil)—Religious life and customs.
4. Rio de Janeiro (Brazil)—Social life and customs.
I. Title.
BL2592.U5H35 2009
299.6'72098153—dc22
2009012684

Designed and typeset by Mina Yamashita.
Cover designed by Melissa Tandysh
Cover photograph courtesy of Getty Images
Text composed in Adobe Garamond Pro, a typeface by
Robert Slimbach combining elements of Garamond and Granjon.
Display set in Origami Std designed by Carl Crossgrove.

Contents

Acknowledgments

In the Umbanda religion that is the subject of this book, it is often said that without the trickster spirit Exu, one can do nothing. While any debt I may owe to Exu must remain a private matter, I will say that without my family, friends, professors, and colleagues, and without the generosity of my Umbanda friends, I could not have written this book.

To my family—my parents, Jewell and Norman, my brothers Doug and Greg—I am indebted for a lifetime of love, support, and wisdom. My mother passed away several months after I began writing this book; knowing she would never have the joy of reading it, I wrote it all the more with her in mind. An extra thanks to Doug and his wife Joanna, who read an earlier version of the manuscript and gave excellent editorial and critical advice. As family to be thanked I also count my former wife, Lisa, to whom I am forever, and affectionately, indebted.

In Brazil, Professor Gilberto Velho of the Graduate Studies Program at the Federal University of Rio de Janeiro was unfailingly generous and helpful. He gave me excellent advice and full access to the resources of the program, including the excellent dissertations from which I learned so much. Equally generous was my colleague Clarice Mota de Novaes, who gave freely her hospitality, advice, and introductions to individuals who would play key roles in my research.

Though it has been many years since they taught me, I benefit every day from the teaching of several superb professors. Dennis McGilvray introduced me to interpretive, psychological, and semiotic approaches to anthropology during my undergraduate studies at the University of Colorado. I was equally fortunate at the University of Texas at Austin.

In the anthropology department, Greg Urban, who supervised my dissertation, gave extraordinary guidance and encouragement, in addition to providing a deep grounding in semiotics and linguistic theory. James Brow, Richard Adams, Henry Selby, and Steven Feld each contributed in unique ways to both my theoretical development and to how I conceive of my roles as anthropologist, teacher, and mentor. From the history department, Richard Graham helped me to see the broad patterns that have shaped Brazil, while Sandra Lauderdale Graham encouraged me to look through the big lens of social theory to see the fine details of lived experience.

I thank the many friends who have been so supportive during the writing of this book. It is best not to list them all, but two in particular I must single out: Constance Iglesias and Lisa Phillips, for their love and support over many years. I also want to thank my friend and former student, Margaret Schugart, and my friend Luciana Castro, for their encouragement during the writing. And I thank my students, who have asked important questions that might never have occurred to me, while brightening my days with their good humor, curiosity, and energy.

I am grateful for the generous award of a Fulbright-Hays Doctoral Dissertation Research Fellowship that supported my longest period of research in 1990–91.

I thank the countless people in Rio de Janeiro who were not the subjects of my research, people that I encountered every day, on the buses, the sidewalks, on the beaches, in the cafes, in government offices, in stores, who, almost without exception, treated me with wonderful kindness and warmth.

Finally, I thank the many Umbanda friends who shared their rituals, beliefs, and stories. To protect their privacy, I do not name any of them in these acknowledgments, and in the text their names have been changed. Without them, of course, this book could not exist. More importantly, they have given me something beyond words, beyond measure. I cannot repay that, but I hope in some small way this book can honor their gift.

Introduction

This book is about the spiritual beliefs and practices of various people that I came to know in Rio de Janeiro beginning in 1986. These people, who come from all walks of life, all colors and classes, practice a religion that most North Americans would find strange, even bizarre. It is a religion in which the spirits of old slaves and Brazilian Indians speak through the mouths of mediums in trance.[1] It is a religion that worships African gods but often calls them by the names of Catholic Saints, and it is a religion that embraces the concepts of karma and reincarnation, Christian charity, and a belief in the efficacy of both modern science and ancient magic. Through numerous journeys to Rio spanning nearly a decade—the longest visit, in 1990–91, lasting over a year, with others of two and three months at a time—I had the opportunity to spend countless hours attending rituals and festivals, talking to participants and non-participants alike, asking questions, and immersing myself in a world that to this day enchants, disturbs, delights, and fascinates me.

The religion is known as Umbanda. That simple statement is barely on the page, and I already need to qualify it. Most of the people I know who practice Umbanda, when asked their religion, will answer: *Sou católica* (I am Catholic). Indeed, many of the people who come to Umbanda do not do so to worship and do not exhibit religious attitudes such as awe, reverence, and wonder. They come, instead, hoping that those spirits of old slaves and Brazilian Indians will use their powers to fix the problems in their lives. But for many other people, Umbanda is the path to a rich and deep spiritual life, a fellowship of faith and service, and a guiding star in a sometimes dark and difficult world. And, as we will see, Umbanda takes many forms; referring to it in the singular masks differences as striking as day and night.

Umbanda is a relatively new religion, dating to the first decade or so of the twentieth century. Its beginnings are to be found in Rio de Janeiro and that city's surrounding urban areas. There, many Afro-Brazilians—some the descendents of slaves, others ex-slaves finally freed by the abolition act of 1888—practiced versions of the religions brought by them and their ancestors from Africa. These Afro-Brazilian religions, which if anything are now stronger and more vital and popular than ever before, faced police oppression and were stigmatized as superstitious, immoral, and, most damning of all in such a racist environment, as legacies of "barbaric" Africa. At this same time, a French import called *espiritismo* (spiritism) enjoyed wide popularity among the well to do (and white) elite. When innovators combined elements of Afro-Brazilian religions and espiritismo, Umbanda was born.[2] It proved to be highly adaptable. During the twentieth century, Umbanda grew tremendously in popularity, attracting millions of participants, mainly in Rio de Janeiro and São Paulo, but also in other urban areas throughout the country.[3]

In writing this book, I seek to accomplish three tasks. First, I seek to place the spiritual beliefs and practices that I observed within the broader contexts of Brazilian culture and history. How has the contested, ambivalent, and lingering drama of race and racism shaped Umbanda? What do these spirits of old slaves and Brazilian Indians (and cowboys, criminals, innocent children, and charming ladies of the night, among other characters) tell us about the Brazilian myths of national identity and history, and how do they speak to the realities of contemporary life? Second, I locate Umbanda within the lives of those who practice it, to answer such questions as: What brings people to Umbanda? What does it mean to them, what does it do for them, how does it change their lives? And, finally, I describe this world or, rather, these worlds of Umbanda that so enchant, disturb, delight, and fascinate me. These three tasks are not at all separable, really. Those who practice it live within the imagined worlds Umbanda creates; those worlds are constructed within and against historical and cultural contexts, and through the agency of those who live in them.

My approach has been local, ethnographic, experiential, and personal. This is not a comprehensive account of Umbanda by any means; even if such an account were possible, I am not the one to write it. Instead, I focus on what I saw, heard, and experienced over the course of a decade of research. These experiences immersed me in worlds of spirits and forces, rhythms and songs, prayers and magic, power and whimsy. I have tried to give readers some sense of those imagined, image-filled worlds because, in large measure, these are what Umbanda *is*, and is about. Too often, in my view, we anthropologists, in our (necessary) efforts at constructing generalized models of structures and patterns, flatten these worlds and drain the very blood out of the life we have been privileged to witness.[4] Theoretically, my approach is informed by phenomenologists, such as Edmund Husserl, Martin Heidegger, and Maurice Merleau-Ponty, in taking lived, first person experience as both the point of departure for and the eventual destination of inquiry. It is also grounded in what the anthropologist Michael Jackson, following the lead of the American pragmatic philosopher and psychologist William James, called "radical empiricism."[5] Empiricism posits an observer, objectively looking out upon a field of events that exists independently of her or his presence. Radical empiricism turns this notion on its head. I have no doubt as to the independent existence of what I observe but, in the spirit of radical empiricism, I know that my observations cannot help but be filtered through my own subjectivity; that I am not only an observer, but a participant whose presence certainly affects events; and, finally, that whatever generalizations we can make about the world—or about Umbanda—our observations are always grounded in particular moments, particular places, particular points of view. Thus, this is not so much a catalogue of Umbanda beliefs and practices as it is a reflective account of my encounter with them.

But this book is not just a glimpse, however vivid or not, of the Umbanda experience. It is also a work of anthropological analysis. The spiritual beliefs and practices I observed, the enchanted worlds I was led into, are social facts, the products of historical forces and cultural contexts, and as an anthropologist it is my job to explicate those. The historical forces include slavery, the persistence of racism, and inequalities of wealth and power. The cultural contexts include symbols, myths, memories, habits, and tastes, that whole web of meaning in which all human life is captured. Here my goal has been not so much to "explain" Umbanda, but more to "read" it, to make sense of it, to interpret what I observed and experienced. I call that "anthropological analysis"; what it boils down to is: this is what I saw, this is what (I think) it means, and why.[6]

As social facts—a concept I take from Emile Durkheim, one of the founding figures of modern sociology and anthropology—these spiritual beliefs and practices have force, like the facts of economy or geography or physics.[7] A spirit may have no material weight, and to a skeptic no reality whatsoever, but to one who believes, a spirit is a real and weighty fact, one to be taken into account. While I carry through with Durkheim's suggestion that the goal of analysis is to abstract these social facts from their individual manifestations, to inductively arrive at the underlying rules and categories of Umbanda belief and practice, I am equally concerned to show how these social facts of belief and practice play out, and are played with, in the lives of Umbandistas. Mine is a two-fisted anthropology: One the one hand, analytic social science; on the other, humanistic description.

In writing this book I have been guided by four major assumptions. The first is the familiar view that religion, Umbanda included, serves important cognitive and normative functions or, in simpler language, provides a description of how the world (or the cosmos, if you prefer) is and how human beings ought to be within it. This perspective was most elegantly presented by Clifford Geertz in an essay that has become a touchstone in the anthropology of religion. Geertz's perspective risks overemphasis on beliefs at the expense of ritual and practice—a persistent bias in religious studies—but Umbanda does in fact spin forth an elaborate cosmology, and so I pay much attention to it while paying full attention to ritual and practice.[8]

The second assumption is that Umbanda is indeed practice, an arena for active doing. Through Umbanda real people deal with the real concerns of life. People seek out the spirits for help with sickness, romance, and employment, protection from rivals, relief from emotional pain, and all kinds of practical, concrete problems. But in addition, many, like religious seekers everywhere, look to Umbanda for meaning, a way to live, shelter from the storm, a community within which to be and to do, a space for what we might call self-actualization. These doings and projects, therefore, are for me a major concern.

The third assumption I call "phenomenological." William James, the psychologist and philosopher I referred to earlier regarding radical empiricism, wrote a book entitled *The Variety of Religious Experience*.[9] The phrase underlines the experiential dimension of religion. Beliefs and rituals, worldviews and ethics, projects and practice are all important, but religion is something people *experience*. It is felt, smelled, heard, sung, danced; it is poetry, metaphor, moods, emotions, ecstasy, and terror.[10] It is lived and, when we ignore the shape and texture of experience, we turn religion into an abstraction. Umbanda is not an abstraction for those who live it; it is enveloping experience, and it comes in a variety of forms. This book conveys the variety of religious experiences I encountered in Umbanda.

The fourth assumption is sociological. Religion is belief, it is ritual, it is practice, it is experience, but these always occur within social and historical contexts. The great sociologist Max Weber, with his sweeping and yet nuanced examination of how religions such as Hinduism and Calvinist Protestantism are shaped by, and shape, economy, politics, ideology, and social institutions is the model, acknowledged or not, for practically every sociological or anthropological discussion of religion since.[11] My efforts are in comparison quite limited, but I do believe that Umbanda must be approached as the product of a society that knew slavery, knows racism, exhibits great inequalities of wealth and power, and has undergone tremendous change during Umbanda's century or so of existence. And further, I believe that the "doings and projects" of the people I discuss relate not only to their personal, private contexts, but to the larger social contexts within which they live their lives.

Umbanda, as I have said, takes strikingly different forms and is practiced by a wide range of people: black, white, and in between; rich, poor, and in between. In doing my ethnographic research I sampled the range of this diversity. One of the people you will meet is Dona Luciana, an Umbanda priestess from an old and wealthy family, who, when I first met her in 1986 presided over a small group of Umbandistas, all white and middle class, who met weekly in her apartment.[12] I spent some time with another small group (members of the Tent of Tupinambá, named for one of the Indian spirits), mostly black and brown and lower income, in the sprawling slum of Rocinha. At yet another, much larger center, the House of Father John (Father John is the spirit of an old slave, mythical founder of the center), participants and visitors ranged from the wealthy—a lawyer, a highly successful businessman and his family, among others—through the middle and working classes, to the very poor. And at the House of Saint Benedict (the patron saint of Black slaves, I was told), participants were all white, the well-off members of the professional and commercial upper middle class.

These groups also represent an important dimension of ritual and aesthetic diversity in Umbanda. The House of Father John and the Tent of Tupinambá exemplify the African roots of Umbanda. Yoruban and Angolan words pepper many of the songs that praise and call down the spirits, while some are sung entirely in these African languages (which no one at either place speaks). African drums and African rhythms summon the spirits, and the African gods—the orixás—are celebrated in annual festivals and nourished with the blood of sacrificial birds and animals. But there are no drums at the House of Saint Benedict; drums, they say there, are "primitive," blood sacrifice a "barbaric" practice. The orixás are redefined; at the House of Saint Benedict, they are conceived of as pure frequencies of spiritual energy, not the mythical deities of an African homeland. Between these two poles, closer really to the House of Saint Benedict, is the Umbanda of Dona Luciana. There are no drums, but that is because she practices in her apartment; drums would disturb the neighbors. But years ago, when she had her own Umbanda center in a large house, she had drummers. She celebrates the orixás, and makes offerings to them—but there are no blood sacrifices, no throats are cut, the offerings instead are of flowers and ribbons, champagne and rosewater. This polarity, between what I will call Afro-Brazilian Umbanda and White Umbanda (the latter term used by those who practice it), is a major focus of my anthropological analysis, and in it I "read" ideologies of race, racism, and antiracism in the ritual aesthetics and spiritual discourse of Umbanda. At the same time, of course, I connect these readings to the social positioning of participants.[13]

This book is written, for the most part, at a very local, personal scale. That is the scale at which I learned about how Umbanda works, and what it means, in the lives of the individuals I came to know, and it is at that scale that I tell their stories. It is from that location that Umbanda is experienced, by participants and by me; and it is only on that scale, detailed and concrete, that I, as a writer, can hope to convey what it looks and feels and sounds like. I have largely built this book around vignettes: my stories and participants' stories. I hope this makes it vivid and engaging, but I also chose this strategy for epistemological reasons, based on a realistic conception of the limits of anthropological observation. I cannot pretend that I achieved anywhere close to a thorough sampling of Umbanda. I saw what I saw because I happened to be where I was when I saw it. I'll never know what I didn't see when I wasn't there at the thousands of Umbanda centers I never visited. I learned a tremendous amount from a relatively small number of people who, due to their unique constellations of temperament, experience, loquacity, reflectivity, and the simple fact of liking me (or at least finding me interesting), enjoyed telling me their stories and teaching me what they knew. I heard far less from those more numerous people who were reticent or from the (hopefully) few who found me off-putting. Of course, what I saw and heard and experienced was filtered through who I am, through the baggage and biases and preconceptions that anyone acquires growing up in their culture and that the anthropologist hopefully becomes aware of through experience and critical reflection. My observations were not only filtered, but affected, by my presence: certainly no less than and probably far more so than with physics, in anthropology the act of observation affects what is observed.[14] And certainly I cannot tell all I saw; to write, a writer must select what she or he thinks counts. I believe this partiality and subjectivity is true of most anthropological fieldwork; we are just witnesses at ground level. We can pretend to objectivity, to distance, to the eagle eye view of the social scientist, but it's really just pretend for most of us, certainly in my case.[15] Hopefully, by writing at a personal scale, you will get a sense of where I might see clearly and where possibly not; a sense of what counts to me and what might not. I rely on you to read this for what it is, not the big book of Umbanda, but simply my book of my journeys within Umbanda. So, here is some of what I saw, some of what I experienced, some of what I was told, and some of what I make of it.

CHAPTER I

The Invisible World

There is the material, and there is the spiritual; in Umbanda we work with the spiritual, on the side of good, in the path of light and truth, serving our guides, the messengers from the Beyond, above all our greatest guide Jesus Christ, Oxalá.[1]

Those were the words of Hector, as I remember them now, twenty-two years later. Hector, himself a guide and messenger from Beyond (indeed, Hector, who spoke through my friend Ronaldo, identified himself as an ancient Greek mariner from some few thousand years ago), had interesting things to say about the spiritual, how it differed from the material. For example, in the spiritual dimension, the limitations of time and space and physics that rule our material lives do not apply. Hector could be there, at that moment, in Brazil, and at the same time a continent away giving healing energy to an ailing relative of mine, and, still in that same moment, feeling the salt breeze of the Aegean three thousand years ago. "The material and the spiritual are radically different, but they coexist, indeed they are intimately linked," Hector said. Take the body. Your body, he explained, is material, composed of water and various elements, arranged into tissues and organs according to instructions coded in the DNA, following the plan of the creator; it is visible, palpable, material, and mortal. Coexistent with that material body is a spiritual body, invisible to the material eye, without substance, yet just as real, and vulnerable to spiritual injury and contamination, just as the material body is vulnerable to germs and traffic accidents. The two are separate—indeed, the spiritual body survives the death of the material body, returning at that moment to its true home, the astral—and yet, in life, the spiritual body and the material body are intimately linked. Spiritual pathology can sicken the body, make the mind nervous, the heart depressed; diseases of the body can affect the spirit, leaving it in need of cleansing and strengthening. And Hector would go on to talk about the astral, the realm of pure spirit and vibration, where one goes after leaving this material existence, if only to eventually return to this vale of tears.

This chapter presents a brief sketch of Umbanda cosmology. I write it uneasily, because I know that my sketch is partial and because I know that it is a sketch of an abstraction, a composite. There is no one, authoritative source of Umbanda cosmology. "Cosmology" is such a grand word, and indeed it denotes a grand thing, a theory of how the universe is, where we fit in, where it is all going. I'm tempted to present it as such, as a grand, abstract, unified system. But that misleads; that is not how Umbanda cosmology looks on the ground, but rather how it looks to a certain cast of mind. Different Umbandistas say different things, at different times, for different reasons, about what Hector calls the spiritual. Even the same Umbandista can say different things, even contradictory things, about the shape and purpose and ultimate meaning of the cosmos, from one context to the next—for example, she might at one moment refer to the African god Ogum as Saint George and, in the next, as a vibration and a force of nature, having nothing at all to do with the Catholic saint. I suspect much of the cosmology goes unsaid, implicit in Umbanda practices. So what I present here is a sketch, a *bricolage*, made up from bits and pieces of what people have explicitly said and implied, and from what I have inferred from their sayings and doings. It is a sketch that comes from sketches, from the etchings of what I have understood or thought I understood from what I have seen and heard. Anyone can contradict it, and anyone would be right to do so, because I am sure that for much of what I present, alternate interpretations can be found. But that can't be helped. I present my sketch of Umbanda cosmology, inferred from sketches, in sketches.[2]

A SPANISH DANCER

"¡Buenas noches! ¡Buenas Noches! ¡Ha, Ha, Ha!"

Peals of laughter cascaded from the open door of Dona Luciana's bed-room, washing over the handful of guests waiting in the living room. A middle-aged woman stood and shook out the hems of her designer jeans; another, I noticed, squeezed her eyes closed and quickly mouthed a silent wish. More high pitched laughter, a clickety-clack of wood on wood, and Ronaldo appeared at the bedroom door.

"Mari-Carmen has arrived, and she wishes to greet everyone in this house." With that, Ronaldo stepped aside, bowed with a sweeping gesture of his left arm, as if to clear the way, and ducked back as Dona Luciana, dressed in a tight, fancy, old yellow silk dress, Spanish leather shoes, a yellow rose in her hair, rings on her fingers, and castanets in her hands came twirling through the doorway and into the living room, heels clicking like tap shoes on the wooden floor. "¡Buenas noches! ¡Ha, Ha Ha! ¡Bienvenidos amigos! Mari-Carmen está lista para servir a mis amigos aqui esta noche!" (Good evening! Ha, Ha, Ha! Mari-Carmen is ready to serve my friends here tonight!).

Mari-Carmen, who visits the home of Dona Luciana on the first Monday of every month, is a spirit of the kind known as *pomba-gira*. Some say that the name pomba-gira comes from a Bantu word *bombomgira*, which refers to the class of spirits known as exus. In Portuguese, a pomba is a pigeon, and gira, in the parlance of Afro-Brazilian religion, is the circle dance with drumming and singing that celebrates and calls down the spirits and the African gods. Pomba, in regional slang, is also a euphemism for the vulva. So the name resonates on multiple levels.

The allusion to the vulva is certainly apt. Pomba-giras are female entities, the spirits of women—some were prostitutes; all have life stories placing them outside the boundaries of strict Catholic morality and bourgeois propriety. When they visit Umbanda centers, their mediums put on fancy dresses, usually red and black, and glittery costume jewelry. The pomba-giras are ribald, sexy in a campy way. They flirt, they wink, they vamp; their speech is peppered with double entendres and euphemisms. They laugh easily and often and, when they laugh, it is said that one should make a wish, which makes for lots of wishes in a pomba-gira session. Though they do neither at Dona Luciana's, in many Umbanda centers the pomba-giras drink and smoke. The drink is usually false champagne; the popping of a cork brings peals of laughter from the spirits. Many smoke regular, commercial, filter-tipped cigarettes, sometimes through an elegant holder, stylish and sexy in an old-movie kind of way. There are variations; there are a few pomba-giras who swig *cachaça*, a raw, pungent, cheap, and potent rum; one of my favorite pomba-giras puffs on very thin, long cigars, while another, the loudest laugher of any I've met, smokes two or three or more cigarettes at once. Sometimes she even uses both hands, two cigarettes between the index and middle fingers of her left hand, two more in her right, puffing away at a manic rate.

As I say, pomba-giras have life stories. Most are set in Brazil, either in colonial times or in the nineteenth century. Mari-Carmen's story is not. Mari-Carmen hails from Andalusia—that is why she greets us in Spanish. Mari-Carmen was a flamenco dancer, a young woman of the night, of parties and gaiety and sensuality. Tragically, she fell in love with a man from the right side of the tracks, a young aristocrat, "almost a prince" as she puts it. Their love was passionate and true, but of course he had to marry within his rank. Mari-Carmen, heart broken, turned to drink and affairs— she might have even had an abortion, she's hinted at it a few times—and died in the dregs. Mari-Carmen's story is unique, but it follows a common pattern: a basically good woman, corrupted (in part by factors beyond her control), winds up on the path to ruin. The road to ruin seems to be paved with good parties, boisterous fun, cachaça, champagne, cigarettes, lusty sex, and other transgressive delights. But of course it ends badly, a nod no doubt to conventional morality, which pomba-gira mocks. The party girl must pay the price. That is why pomba-gira comes to Umbanda: to earn redemption, to evolve morally and spiritually (which are really the same), a central tenet of Umbanda practice and belief. But before discussing this aspect of pomba-gira, we must first place her within Umbanda's cast of spiritual characters.

VISITORS FROM THE BEYOND

In Umbanda belief, every living person has a spirit, and this spirit survives the death of the body. While Umbandistas often define the spirit in abstract terms, for example as a vibration with its own unique frequency, the spirits manifested in the performances of mediums are far from abstract; they exhibit personalities; they are endowed with emotions, life histories, values, moral qualities, quirks, mannerisms of speech and gesture, and names.

The spirits of the dead or the not yet born reside in the realm of pure nonmateriality. Some of my friends referred to this as the *além*, the "Beyond" (as in "beyond the grave"), others as the astral, or *plano astral* (astral plane). Ronaldo described it as a kind of parallel universe, no "place" in particular, but everywhere, simultaneously. On the other hand, Umbandistas, including Ronaldo, often endow this realm with spatiality, with location; for example, in a number of hymns, the home of the spirits is called Aruanda, which, like many ritual words in Umbanda, has African resonance, sounding much like Luanda, the capital of Angola, or Rwanda, in Central Africa. A hymn that evokes the war god Ogum tells of his coming from Aruanda to save children of Umbanda; when it is time for him to go, the verse is transformed into a report of Ogum's leaving for Aruanda. As with spirits themselves, many Umbandistas use abstract language in defining the spiritual realm—ether, cosmos, energy, and so on—but in the poetic language of hymns and the words of spirits speaking through mediums, imagery endows Aruanda with sensual substance. For example, one hymn tells us that the singer saw, in the blue morning sky, a star shining—the home of the African deity Oxalá, located in Aruanda. In other hymns the spiritual realm takes the form of Indian villages in the forests; again, poetic imagery imparting shape and sentiment to the abstract and unseeable, "so that our limited minds have something to grab hold of"—that is how Ronaldo explained the seeming contradiction between his definition of Aruanda as the nonmaterial realm of pure spirit and the strikingly sensual images of village, sky, and forest that evoke its presence.

Aruanda, or the astral, is a populous place. The spirits of everyone not now living are there, as are the African deities, the orixás, discussed in a later chapter. It may be a realm devoid of material, ethereal, outside the structures of normal time and space, but it is not without social organization and hierarchy. A spirit belongs to one of a number of legions, also known as *falanges*, such as the Legion of the Mermaids, or the Legion of the Guarani (referring to a broad family of indigenous Brazilian peoples, the Tupi-Guarani), or the People of Mozambique, and so on. Each of these legions is associated with a number of other legions to form a *linha*, or line, under the direction of a superior spiritual entity, in most case one of the orixás, such as Iemanjá the sea goddess. Within these groupings there are further subdivisions, and individual spirits are ranked according to degree of spiritual merit. Even in the Infinite, it seems, everyone has her place, her particular niche on the great organizational chart of the Beyond.

While most of the lines are associated with an orixá, an African god, Mari-Carmen belongs to the Oriental Line, as do many other spirits that Dona Luciana works with. Included in the Oriental Line are, among others, Chinese, Japanese, Eskimos, Egyptians, Phoenicians, some Native Americans, Romans and Gaels, and other Europeans: spirits may be immaterial but race and blood, it seems, are essential categories, even in the Beyond. Spirits in the Oriental Line, according to Dona Luciana, are distinguished by their intelligence, refinement, subtlety, and taste: Mari-Carmen, Dona Luciana points out by way of illustration, would never engage in the over-the-top ribaldry (*grosseirias*) of most pomba-giras. "And just look at those clothes she had me buy for her! How elegant—they cost me a fortune!"

A TAXONOMY OF SPIRITS

Refined though she may be, Mari-Carmen is hardly near the top of the moral hierarchy of spirits. Pomba-giras, like their male counterparts the exus, are certainly beloved and essential to Umbanda—essential because, as they say, "without exu, nothing is done," and beloved because exus and pomba-giras, like most of us (the interesting ones among us anyway), have their gluttonous, lustful, slothful, envious, wrathful sides and, besides, they are wonderfully humorous. But they are certainly not saints.

Spirits are ranked according to their "degree of evolution." Besides their regimentation into legions and lines, the spiritual entities that visit Umbanda centers (and some that do not, such as the Catholic saints), also fit into a small number of categories ranked from highest to lowest. Although in practice things are more flexible and ambiguous, the scheme itself is simple and can be briefly described, beginning at the top:

Orixás (and Saints)

The orixás are the African deities, variously presented as mythological characters, forces of nature, vibrations, and essences, which are identified with certain Catholic Saints. These are the most highly evolved spirits; many Umbandistas maintain that they are too elevated to deal directly with earthly beings and so they send instead their emissaries, the caboclos and the *pretos velhos* (literally, old blacks), to do their work among the human beings who come to Umbanda.

Caboclos

These are generally the spirits of Brazilian Indians, though they need not be. One of Dona Luciana's caboclos, for example, is a young Portuguese girl, while another is a Spanish crusader. They are strong, brave, moral, and very spiritual—in short, "highly evolved," as Dona Luciana puts it. They often serve as emissaries of the orixás, even sometimes as stand-ins for the orixás. (I discuss the caboclos and their relationship to the orixás at length in Chapter 5.)

Pretos Velhos

These are usually the spirits of old slaves, though, again, not always; one of Dona Luciana's pretos velhos is an old Hindu woman with paralyzed legs. I discuss this category at greater length in Chapter 4.

Crianças (spirits of infants and young children)

While the spirits of old slaves and Indians work hard at giving advice and protection, the crianças, like living children, are valued not for their practical contributions but, rather, for the joy, vitality, humor, spontaneity, and naïve wisdom they bring to a weary and worried grown-up world. Except for the annual "birthday party" for the child spirits, which is held on the feast day for the child martyr saints Cosmas and Damian, their appearances tend to be unscheduled—after all, people come to Umbanda primarily to seek aid and advice and what do children know of such adult trials and tribulations as money worries, backstabbing coworkers and toxic bosses, alcoholic husbands and cheating wives? When the child spirits come, it is usually at the end of long sessions in which adult problems have left a cloud of gloom, tension, and tiredness. First one, then another and another medium will break into giggles and pouts and baby talk, nursery rhymes, and the whole kaleidoscope of childish gestures. Pacifiers, toys, candy, and soft drinks may be brought out; the mood is light, joyous. The adults who are not receiving the child spirits play with them, indulge them, dote on them, give them coins, puzzle out their malapropisms and baby talk. The child spirits have names—cute-sifications formed by adding the diminutive "inho" or "inha" to a regular name, as in "Jureminha" (Little Jurema), in just the way adults affectionately refer to living children—and they have personalities and histories. Dona Luciana's Pedrinho, for example, is a somewhat hyperactive, mischievous, and cheerful little boy, adept with a toy slingshot, forever young by way of falling out of a tree and cracking open his skull at around the age of seven. Her Jureminha, by contrast, is a little Indian princess who sits by an invisible waterfall, waving two ribbon-festooned sticks as she sings in a language none of us can understand, but surely her song brings luck and happiness to those who sit at her feet.

The crianças are rooted in the West African tradition of the twin child entities, the Ibejis. Twin births are anomalous, due in part to their rarity but perhaps due more to the challenges they pose to identity, the boundaries of self and other, and nature and culture. The Ibejis are contradictory in other ways; they are represented as children, yet conceived as powerful entities, innocent and naïve yet wise. In the more African strains of Umbanda, as at the House of Father John, for example, child spirits—referred to as erés—play a very important role in initiation. During the period of seclusion, the initiate is frequently possessed by the erés, who, like living children, learn new things quickly, especially new words and meanings, and who, again like children, are not yet estranged as adults are from the enchanted realms of spirituality, imagination, and play. Initiation, too, is a rebirth, and surely there can be no birth without a child. Thus, the eré.

Onto the African roots of the Ibejis, Umbanda grafts a flourishing Euro-Brazilian cultural foliage, almost obscuring the original form. They are represented as the child martyrs, saints Cosmas and Damian. While Cosmas and Damian are indeed twins, the actual spirits mediums receive rarely are. The crianças resonate with the folk Catholic notion of little angels, children who die while still in a state of innocence and grace. They are little cowboys, Indians, and plantation slave children, princesses, babies and toddlers, and little boys with slingshots; they crave sweets and covet toys; they play pranks, throw fits, and laugh—the sacred, awesome mystery of the African twins transformed into bouncy, sometimes bratty, Brazilian children.

And yet for all the candy and pacifiers and pranks and baby talk, the crianças speak to important issues of need and want, joy and hurt, hope and loss. For example, one September 27th night, the feast day for Cosmas and Damian, I spent the evening at Dona Luciana's, attending a party for the child spirits. It proved to be a much pleasanter affair than another child spirit party I had attended at the House of Father John. At Father John's, I had spent an exhausting afternoon helping out with crowd control. Literally hundreds of children, mostly poor, accompanied by their parents or other adults, had flocked to the center for a shot at their share of the dolls, stuffed bears, action figures, balloons, toy trucks, bulldozers, and whatnot contributed for the event by the wealthier friends of the center.[3] Toys and food—cake and candy, of course, but also nourishing stuff, including *caruru*, a deeply filling, mildly spicy stew of shrimp, okra, peppers, and onion, as well as fruit and beans. The crowd grew, literally, for hours, crowded, cramped, milling, impatient. My job was to gently keep people back until, after what seemed (but wasn't) several hours of drumming and dancing, the mediums finally received their child spirits, played and cavorted for awhile; the living children could then take the stage and get their toys and, later, a meal. It was tense and exhausting. The floor where I stood was a few feet above ground level, where the crowd waited impatiently. I was looking out onto a turbulent sea of want and need, though in this case maybe the two can't be readily separated—poor children wanting toys, poor adults needing something for their children, everyone needing food. I had anticipated a happy occasion—a celebration of the spirits, giving gifts to children, sharing food with all. The festivities began with a homily concerning the Umbanda value of charity, of generosity to those in need; about the joy of children, to be celebrated on this day; warm thanks to all those who contributed materially to make this day possible. Certainly it was generous of those who contributed what surely was several thousand dollars worth of toys and food. But looking out over that restless, wanting crowd, children dependent on generosity for that which simple economic justice should provide, I felt badly, resentful of the structures that allow some few to feel generous while others are forced to rely on charity, ashamed of the privilege that made me a gatekeeper whom they respectfully (if resentfully) obeyed. I just wanted it to end. The afternoon, of course, would. The oppression prettied up by the balloons and toys—not in my lifetime, I suppose.

But this night at Dona Luciana's comfortable apartment there should not be any painful, unexpected reminders of the brutal facts of Brazil's savage inequalities of wealth. The bedroom had been lavishly prepared for the birthday party, the bed folded away into the armoire, brightly colored balloons festooned the dresser and in front of the altar were heaped big fluffy marshmallow candies, chocolate bunnies, Kraft Caramels, lollipops and soft drinks, a toy soccer ball, a couple of dolls, and a teddy bear. Several regular visitors were there when I arrived, but no children—not surprisingly, most of the regulars are women well into their middle ages and their children have grown into adulthood or adolescence. Soon enough Dona Luciana and Ronaldo and Joana retired to the bedroom, received their child spirits, and the party began. The "children" played with the toys, gorged on candy and *guaraná*,[4] and managed to smear their faces with icing and chocolate. At one point, Dona Luciana received the spirit of a very young child and sucked on a whole string of pacifiers. I must admit that I found these encounters with child spirits tedious, though intellectually fascinating when seen from various psychological and psychoanalytic perspectives. To literally get in touch with the inner child, to escape the cares and responsibilities of adult life, to be pampered and catered to, to smear oneself with candy and cake, while careening through the labile emotions of childhood, protected from any sense of shame or embarrassment at such release by the belief that, after all, it is a spirit, not the self, acting out, and the positive sanctioning of the acting out—not my cup of tea, but I could understand the draw of these things. As I somewhat insincerely fawned over these "children" cavorting in the bodies of a man and a woman nearly my age (late thirties, at the time) and a woman in her seventies, I longed for this childish celebration, too, to be over.

And then something unexpected happened. Dona Luciana received another spirit, a child that no one knew. "Who are you?" Dona Luciana, or rather the criança, looked at his feet, mumbled, sounding very small and frightened. We offered him chocolate, but he spat it out. (As it happens, Dona Luciana is allergic to chocolate, as I would learn later.) Hilda offered the criança a piece of cake, which it devoured with barely a chew, and then a little glass of guaraná, gulped down in a swallow. Hilda patiently coaxed out his story. Rogério it seems was a little poor kid. Abandoned before he could even remember, he lived on the streets, begging and stealing from garbage cans, living with a little group of urchins who knew the normal things of childhood—protecting and affectionate parents, candy and cake, toys and carefree joy—only vicariously, from outside looking in (much as he was doing here). And how did he come to be a little angel, roaming now the streets of that invisible world? Rogério pressed his lips together, shook his head— he wasn't going to talk about it. "Tell us, Rogério." "No." "Tell us. No one here will hurt you. You're safe with us. You can tell us, Rogério." Eventually it came out. It seems that Rogério and his friends had worn out their welcome with the restaurant and shop owners who complain that homeless kids scare away the respectable folks whose tastes for long lazy lunches and up-to date-fashions pay the bills. These respected businessmen, these men who reputedly hire thugs to protect their businesses and "clean the street," took no liking to little Rogério and his friends. And so some big men came around and put an end to Rogério. (In fact a lot of this "street cleaning" was going on at that time: in a case that made headlines and led the nightly news, several street children were butchered on the steps of the Candalária church in downtown Rio on July 23, 1993, shot as they slept huddled together for warmth against the night chill. Supposedly the children had thrown rocks at passing police cars the day before, provoking the ire of the police officers. Eight children would die for that "crime." The incident galvanized public opinion and brought national and international attention to the plight of Rio's street children. A number of men, including seven policemen, were accused of the killings; two were convicted.)

Unexpectedly, righteously, the real had found its way in. Little Rogério wolfed another piece of cake, and it was time to go.

**_Exus da luz_ (exus of the light, also called _exus batizados_,
baptized exus; includes many of the pomba-giras)**

Mari Carmen is an exu da luz[5]—repentant of her sins, she has seen the
light and seeks redemption and karmic advancement by serving the orixás
and the children of Umbanda. An analogy can be drawn between exus da
luz and souls in purgatory—sinful in life, but not irredeemably so, working off their moral debts in the shadows of earthly existence (though quite
often their sins are mortal ones). That the Catholic cast of penitent souls
served as models for the Umbanda characters cannot be proven, but the
resonances are unmistakably there.

I am often struck by the essential humanity and goodness of these
figures—sinners, even mortal sinners they may have been, but their crimes
stem from human frailty, ambiguous circumstances, even from trying to
achieve right ends through "wrong" means. Ronaldo's exu Caveira (Skull),
for example, was a generous physician, donating his services to the poor,
supporting his charitable work through his practice with a wealthy clien-
tele. Among his patients were aristocratic young women made pregnant
by heartless seducers and rapists—that is, through no fault of their own.
The good doctor would abort their pregnancies, saving their reputations at
the cost of his soul; Caveira reports guilty feelings and dreams of laughing
children who would never be, but says he felt at the time he was doing the
right thing. He now reports seeing the error of his ways, though he doesn't
sound quite convinced.

Or take the exu Tranca Rua (Bar the Street) who works through Seu
Silva, leader of the House of Father John. There are many Tranca Ruas, as
there are many Caveiras, but this is the story Zé told me one night about
Seu Silva's Tranca Rua. It seems that many centuries ago Tranca Rua was
a Catholic priest—not in Brazil, but in the old country. He was a good
priest, devoted to the poor. ("So, he practiced the preferential option for
the poor?" I asked, using the language of liberation theology. "Exactly. The
very same.") He came to see the church and state as partners in oppression, and took up the rebel cause. He fought, he killed, he loved women,

fathered children, and he died condemned for his "sins." From his stirring account and shining eyes, I could see that Zé clearly admired Tranca Rua, a man of courage and passion, champion of justice. Tranca Rua, Zé concluded, was a *real* man, a *true* priest.

Exus das trevas (exus of the shadows)

Exus das trevas are unrepentant spirits, tortured souls who have not seen the light, dangerous entities that afflict and torment the living. Malevolent sorcerers enlist their aid through a whole system of nefarious practices diametrically opposed to Umbanda, known as *Quimbanda*.

Referred to frequently as "obsessors," these spirits are no strangers to Umbandistas. Indeed, many of the people who come seeking relief from terrible luck, emotional pain, alcohol and drug addictions, compulsive behaviors, rage, and so forth, are thought to be victims of these predatory spirits. The obsessor is said to be "leaning" (*encostado*) on the sufferer, pushing, pressuring, twisting the victim's perceptions and emotions, distracting her, darkening her heart—the specific effects vary. The obsessor may be sent by a sorcerer (*feiticeiro*) of Quimbanda on behalf of a rival, a vengeful former friend or lover, or an enemy, for whatever motive. Or it may attack on its own accord, out of resentment toward the living, for the satisfaction of causing another to hurt as it does. Umbanda deals with these matters—often in dramatic, graphic, cathartic fashion.

An example, one episode among innumerable others of its kind: I am sitting in the front row at the House of Father John watching the caboclos (Indian spirits) as they cleanse and counsel and treat the various persons who come for their aid that night. Their voices and the voices of the twenty or so people sitting around and behind me on the benches flow in a soft murmur. Fernando sits behind his drum, quiet, tending to his own thoughts. In one corner, the Cowboy of Time (classed among the caboclo spirits even though he and his fellow cowboys are not at all like the stereotypical noble savages all around them—they are instead hardscrabble, bow-legged, stiff-gaited, bullwhip-cracking in some cases, cowboys) stands in the corner, a hand on one hip, the other hand clutching a big cigar, head cocked to one side, squinting eyes scrutinizing the face of the middle-aged woman telling him her complaint. It is an interesting point that the Cowboy of Time is a he; his medium, though, is a woman. A few feet away, the Indian caboclo Seven Arrows, using a leafy branch, sweeps head to toe, back and front, a young, worried-looking man, fumigates him with the smoke of his cigar, and then leans close to the young man and, at whisper distance, they begin to talk. I cannot hear them, but I can see the tempo of their speaking mouths, the tightness around the young man's mouth, the tension in his gestures. It must be serious business.

My attention wanes and my gaze is drawn to the far corner. The caboclos Coral Snake, White Feather, and Stump Puller are huddled around a young woman. I can barely see her, but I recognize her from earlier. She had been sitting alone on the front bench across the aisle from me, looking sad and worried, as though she might start crying at any minute. Now the three caboclos surround her. Suddenly the knot of white-clad mediums breaks open, as the young woman's arms flail wildly at her side. Her body stiffens and inclines backward; she screams. Stump Puller catches her as she falls back, his body pressed close to avoid her flailing arms. Her physical convulsions quickly subside, giving way to sobs and snarled words. It is the obsessor, the spirit who has been leaning on her, possessing her body. A caboclo that everyone calls simply "The Cowboy" strides up, bullwhip in hand, and stands before the sobbing, shaking woman. "Who are you?" he demands. "Why do you bother my herd? Speak!"

Amid racking sobs, tangled fragments of the obsessor's story emerge. The bits suggest a tormented earthly existence and a violent death. It is not a coherent narrative, and The Cowboy cut it off almost immediately, but I hear the words rape, burning, murder. As so often happens, in this case the obsessor, victimized herself, had turned her pain and rage on the living. The Cowboy beseeched her to seek the path of truth, to leave the past behind. She snarled and blubbered. The Cowboy turned from gentle to forceful, ordering her to leave, leave, to never dare return to torment this young woman. The drummer, whether on his own initiative or in response to some signal from The Cowboy, broke into a rhythm, the mediums began singing, the obsessor sobbed, grew quiet, and presumably left. The woman, drained but now calm, returned to herself. Coral Snake led her back to the corner; they talked for a few minutes—it all looked very calm—she went out back to light a candle, and then returned to the bench across the aisle from me. She sat quietly for a few minutes, then put her shoes back on and walked off into the night. The bad spirit was gone, for now at least, banished to its shadowy corner of the Beyond. I wondered if it would stay away.

REINCARNATION

Living people, Ronaldo tells me, are *espíritos encarnados* (incarnate spirits). To have flesh, substance, to breathe, suffer, and take earthly pleasure is a passing state. The body dies, the spirit lives on, and it eventually returns to inhabit a new body, through which it is given once again the chance to better its karma through earthly endeavor before again returning to Aruanda.

The concepts of reincarnation and karma—the actual words used are *reincarnação* and *karma*, even though the letter K is not in the Portuguese alphabet—entered Umbanda through the Spiritism of Allan Kardec (discussed in Chapter 3). For Ronaldo and Dona Luciana and many other Umbandistas, reincarnation is a centrally important concept. By serving the spirits (and the living who seek their help) in this lifetime, they build up karmic credit. After death, this credit affords them a higher level in the astral, and a better life when they reincarnate. Spirits, too, build karma. Mari-Carmen, and exu Skull, for example, atone for past misdeeds and work toward a brighter spiritual future through their good works in Umbanda.

Beyond pointing to one's spiritual future, reincarnation provides a framework for understanding the present. For example, Dona Luciana strongly suspects that she and I have known each other quite well, for a long time, in some previous life or, more likely, lives. She can't be certain.

Her spirits often tell her a great deal indirectly, by speaking through her when she is in trance, leaving spoken messages with the unentranced to give to her after the session. They also speak to her directly, as when the Bedouin spirit Habib appears to her, late at night as if in a dream, usually as she watches television, to tell her things she needs to know. But the spirits haven't told her about our knowing each other before, and she doesn't remember her own past lives, but she still thinks we have known each other before. "What else could it be? A young man[6] from the United States, a Brazilian grandmother, look at how we immediately connected and how close we've become. As if we've known each other before and for a long time." Dona Luciana went on to suggest that forces are at work that bring kindred spirits together again and again, over the centuries or millennia. "What are the odds that we would meet? Could it just really be coincidence that a friend of a friend would happen to know an Umbanda priestess? What are the odds?" Quite good, it seems, when seen from a perspective in which some persons know each other from before this life; when the dramas and comedies of relationships do not end at death but move on some centuries or millennia later to the next act, and the next; when spiritual time is a river broken by islands and boulders and eddies and backwaters that nonetheless brings its waters back together over and over. That is how Dona Luciana explains it.

Reincarnation is a recurrent theme in Umbanda discourse. Besides providing a way of understanding striking cases of affinity (or enmity) between persons, reincarnation is often invoked as a kind of psychological theory. If childhood experiences, especially traumatic ones, shape us, then past life events must surely play a role; indeed, seemingly anomalous behaviors, puzzling feelings, the mysteries of character, irrational fears, and even tragedy can be read as the leftover lines and scenes from a long-ago drama. An incident from the House of Saint Benedict provides an example.

My notes afterward were sketchy, but my memories of the night, even now, more than a decade later, are detailed and vivid. It was the first Monday of the month, a night set aside for the exu spirits at the House of

Saint Benedict. Seu Gomes would be receiving one of his exus—maybe it would be Marabô, a nineteenth-century French physician relegated to the lower planes of the astral for, among other things, performing abortions (echoes of Mr. Skull) and enjoying an exuberantly decadent nightlife. Or maybe it would be one of Seu Gomes's other tragicomic lowlifes. I was hoping for Marabô, who, much like his medium, is a well-spoken, middle-aged man of some education, a "true scholar" as Dona Linda, leader of the House of Saint Benedict puts it, of "esoteric" Umbanda, versed in such matters as the Cabala, Atlantis, metaphysics, astrology, the quasi-alchemical correspondences of crystals, colors, and vibrations, and the Spiritist cosmology of levels and lines, dimensions and time.

After the opening prayers, the hymns to the orixás, and the songs calling down the spirits, came the main work of the session—the consultations between the spirits and the people who had come for their advice and aid. I waited until all had been served and then sat on the floor facing Gomes. Or, rather, Marabô.

Marabô leaned toward me, I toward him. Our knees were touching, as he wrapped both his hands around mine and squeezed gently, greeting me with a "good evening, my American friend." He snapped his fingers atop my head, around my temples, down my shoulders and arms, above my heart and solar plexus, and then took my hands again. He started to explain about how the *passe*—what he had just done with his snapping fingers—not only cleans and adjusts the astral body that coexists with and envelops our material form, and which, if dirty or unbalanced, can make us ill, or sad, or anxious, but that it also activates the chakras. "Do you know about the chakras?" "Yes, a little, but surely Marabô knows more, so tell me." I settled in for what I expected would be a long treatise on chakras and breath and humors and yoga, full of the (to me) often impenetrable jargon of "esoteric" Umbanda. "We'll talk about chakras some other time," Marabô intoned. "Tonight there is something else." He lit a cigar and studied my face as the smoke wafted around us. "You know what, my American friend, you speak very well; everyone likes to talk to you, ah! You speak our language well, for a foreigner, and you know a lot; my 'horse' [Gomes, the medium receiving Marabô] enjoys his conversations with you so much—music, politics, art, history—a true scholar you are! But you know something, one notes that you stutter a little bit. Not because of our language, I know you do in your own language as well, though we've never spoken together the language of Shakespeare and Emerson [Marabô never misses a chance to gild]. It's not a problem, just a fact, nothing more. But do you know why you stutter?"

Marabô of course was right. I do stutter, not badly, certainly not to the point that it takes any joy out of conversation, or teaching, or the ego-swelling delight of speaking in front of large audiences. Not badly, now, but when I was a child, it was terrible. Marabô was asking if I knew why. Having gone through therapy and devoured all the theories, I felt well prepared as I reviewed current thinking on the matter. After a brief account of neurological bases—cerebral dominance issues, sporadic neural misfiring and so forth, I started in on the etiology of childhood stuttering, self consciousness, avoidance reactions, and so on. But Marabô tapped his finger to his lips, to silence me. "Well yes, that's all very true, I'm sure, quite scientific, you are very learned in this area, but let me tell you why *you* do it. Not that what you said isn't correct, but you're talking about the material. I'm talking about the spiritual side that coexists with the material. Here is why you stutter.

"You are French [I am sure I looked puzzled at this point]. Well, you are American now, but you were French, in another life, a previous incarnation. You do not consciously remember, but the memory lingers, buried deep in your unconscious." Marabô leaned closer. "Buried, but let us see. Close your eyes and try to visualize." Marabô's hands cradled my head, his forehead touching mine. "You lived in Paris, in the eighteenth century. You were a freethinker, *um libre pensante*; you still are today, though you're careful to hide your thoughts these days. You raised the banner of liberty, fraternity, equality! The revolution! The new man! But you were an authentic freethinker and soon turned against repression in the name of freedom, turned against the Jacobins. You spoke against it, you wrote against it. And for your words they arrested you and tortured you, and you had a date with Madame Guillotine! Your words were cut off by the blade that cut off your head. And that is why words sometimes stick in your throat—your throat remembers!"

As Marabô spoke, I visualized, as he had directed. No doubt the imagery had its tangible sources in this-life experience—scenes from old movies and paintings—*Liberty Leading the People* was in there, for instance. And no doubt Marabô's basso profundo voice, eloquent phrasing, the low light, and the suspension of disbelief I employ when reading novels or consulting spirits, contributed to a kind of hypnotic state. Objectivity aside, subjectively this movie playing behind my eyelids felt quite real, a vivid memory, albeit supplemented by perspective shifts that allowed me to see myself from outside, at key moments, such as the date with Madame Guillotine.

"I speak the truth, do I not?" Marabô said after some time. I opened my eyes and looked at him. His eyes were moist. My mood was deep and still far away.

I have thought often over the years about that conversation with Marabô. In part because it so well captures the invisible world that comes to light in Marabô's discourse, an invisible world that in Marabô's telling is vivid, romantic, whimsical, fantastic. It fits Marabô, as it fits his medium, Gomes. I also think of it often because, when I suspend disbelief, it makes sense of some important aspects of my own person. The stuttering, of course. And I like to think of myself as a freethinker, an iconoclast at heart (and what troubles that brought on before I learned the arts of camouflage!). But it also makes some sense in light of my troubled relationship with authority, my wariness of those with power, my anxiety that their favor will turn to menace without warning, all that stemming from an early age. Marabô's myth, when I engage it, illuminates a number of dark corners, big and small: for example, the fascination, dread, and feeling of deep, deep identification as a junior high school student reading *Doctor Zhivago* and *1984*, novels about the fate of those who go against the grain.

And I think of it because it exemplifies how, through those personal, intimate conversations, face to face, hands enfolded in hands, the invisible world is mapped onto the visible, palpable, chaotic, often painful facts of everyday life—thereby lending those facts meaning and grace. I am quite sure, for example, that disorderly, over-excited neurons, and learned anxieties and fears, and so forth, more or less adequately explain the development of stuttering. But Marabô's whimsy suggests something much deeper about its meaning. And about myself.

GLIMPSES OF THE INVISIBLE WORLD

Ronaldo, like other Umbandistas, makes a binary distinction between the material and the spiritual. Referring to the latter as the Beyond, Aruanda, the astral, or the invisible world, might seem to distance the spiritual from the realm of daily life. And yet, for me, the most striking feature of Umbanda is the way that it recasts everyday reality as a kind of looking glass through which one can glimpse the invisible world. I stutter; beneath the tics and repetitions, the Umbanda ear can hear the echoes of repression and terror from a previous life. Repeated episodes of dissociation (as we shall see in the next chapter in the case of Seu Silva), apparently random, are not that at all, or not *just* that—in the spiritually informed Umbanda psychology, they become signs of a calling from the orixás, dramatic scenes from one person's epic spiritual drama, a narrative not only inspirational but richly descriptive of the invisible world.

The invisible world comes to life, becomes real and moving, through the ritual and music and spirit possession but also, and importantly, through imaginative narratives that recast the mundane as spiritual drama. Dona Luciana is an especially masterful maker of such spiritual stories.

It is the second Monday night of the month and, as usual, Dona Luciana is holding a session for the caboclo spirits. There is a heaviness, a tension, in the air, and I don't know why; there are just a few of us there, and we all get along fine. But it is there—a hardness, an edginess. *Mata Virgem* (Virgin Forest), Dona Luciana's caboclo, feels it too. He seems irritated. He turns to Marisa. "Where were you, what did you do, who were you with yesterday?" "With relatives and a friend, Ana." "Ah, that's it." Marisa had picked up a strong, negative energy from this Ana. Ana in turn had picked it up from somewhere else, and it had jumped to Marisa, a good thing, actually, because Mata Virgem was there to deal with it. Mata Virgem performed a passe, running his hands up and down the length of Marisa's body, without touching her, drawing out and discharging the contamination. Nipped in the bud, no lasting harm done.

But still Mata Virgem broods. There is something bad, heavy here, still. He turns to me. Where had I been, who had I seen, on Sunday? I know where this is leading, I think. Dona Luciana knows I go some Sundays to Rocinha, the enormous slum perched on the mountain ridge between Rio's chic South Zone neighborhoods of Gávea and Barra da Tijuca, to attend sessions at the Umbanda center of Dona Rosa. I know Dona Luciana doesn't approve. First, because Rocinha is a slum and, for Dona Luciana, like many middle- and upper-class people, Rio's *favelas* evoke nightmarish images of violence and danger. Second, the Umbanda practiced there is not her style—too "primitive" and too "heavy," which is to say, too Afro-Brazilian, with blood sacrifice and loud drumming and all those other things that one doesn't find in her "elevated" and "evolved" Umbanda. That aside, Dona Luciana repeatedly warns that bad energies and bad spirits are drawn to such *terreiros*, and if the people are not diligent, it can be dangerous. I tell Mata Virgem: "I went to that place in Rocinha."

"But that isn't it. You didn't get it there. Perhaps you were walking home. For sure you were walking along the street, on the sidewalk. Who saw you? Who did you see?" Mata Virgem closed his eyes and pressed his hands to my temples. "Think back. Go back in your mind. It was yesterday, maybe the day before. You are walking along. It is cool, and clear. There, there is a black man, just stopped there. Do you see him?"

I do. It was Saturday afternoon (two days earlier), after lunch. I am walking back to the apartment, passing by the church. It is a pretty church, in an affluent neighborhood. I pass by it every day, several times usually. Some mornings a homeless family is there: a couple of listless, dirty children, sometimes a man, and sometimes a woman with teeth missing and a bewildered look. I think she has an organic brain disorder, but perhaps she is just crazy from chronic hunger and the traumas of street life in Rio. I haven't seen the family for a while, though. I suspect the thugs who provide "security" for the local restaurants and businesses have run them off.

But this Saturday there is this black man. He is drunk, lying out on the sidewalk, dirty, ragged. He is not old, maybe in his thirties. Mata Virgem places his hand on my forehead. "Try to see the man. He looks at you. He has a beard, does he not?"

"I don't remember. When I saw his eyes I looked away."

"Did he look at you?"

"I don't know. Maybe he did."

"I see him now," Mata Virgem says, "I see his eyes. That is the man. That man is dangerous. He is obsessed, surrounded by *sofredores*" (tormented souls who died in agony and cannot give up their pain and their hatred for the living). "That man will die soon and join them. He saw you; he put his eyes on you. When I leave, tell Dona Luciana everything that you and I, Mata Virgem, have said. Tell her to purify this village with the smoke of incense and herbs. She must tell you how to cleanse yourself with a bath made of rose petals in water. You saw this man near where you live? Stay as far away from him as you can."

Mata Virgem cleansed us with passes. After the session was over, I told Dona Luciana what transpired. Dona Luciana fumigated the apartment, spreading a thick, perfumed smoke in every room, every corner. Then we talked. I mentioned that I had seen the man in front of a church. Dona Luciana told me that churches can be spiritually dangerous places, because tormented spirits are attracted by the candles lit for the dead. "So that's why I avoid churches!" I joked. "You laugh," she said, "but this is serious."

The next morning I see that man from my balcony. He is stomping around, talking loudly, as though arguing with someone. People give him plenty of distance as they hurry by. He looks up and I see his bearded face. He is looking at me. I look into his face, and as I hear Mata Virgem's words echo in my brain, I feel like I'm seeing him through Mata Virgem's eyes.

The Umbanda imagination enchants the very landscape. Mountains, the sea, the shore, rivers, waterfalls, swampy patches, a quarry—these are all material, but they are also salient features of the spiritual geography, points where the awesome and the spiritual irrupt into the everyday world.

Dona Luciana tells of a little pilgrimage she and Ronaldo took some years back, to a spot at the end of the beach in Copacabana. Copacabana is a magnet for tourists, who are drawn to its not so clean sands and usually gentle surf, to its *barracas* (beachside stands where one can buy good cold beer in big brown bottles, cokes, iced mate, and snacks) and sidewalk cafes (more cold beer; *caipirinhas* made from crushed limes, sugar, and musty, strong cachaça; french fries; fried sardines or chicken hearts with lots of garlic; in short, the good salty sustenance of sunny leisure), and, only a little way back in the shadows, the brisk sex trade that seems to follow dollars and euros whenever they go south. Beyond all this material front, however, Copacabana is a spiritual place. Before the giant New Year's Eve celebration that draws a million or more to the beach for fireworks and music, thousands of *cariocas* come down to the water to make offerings of flowers and fruit, champagne, coins, and ribbons, and wishes and prayers written on scraps of paper to the African sea goddess Iemanjá. Iemanjá is everywhere in the sea, everywhere the loving mother goddess soothing and protecting her children, but always waiting for the moment to take them home beneath the waves; she is everywhere, but if gods live through the veneration of humans, then especially she lives in the warm waters of Copacabana.

This particular pilgrimage was not specifically concerned with Iemanjá, however, or with the broad swath of her signature beach. It had to do with Xangô, the god of thunder and lightening, of law and justice. Among the most important orixás, if we measure by the attention devoted him in ritual and myth, Xangô is further associated with stone working and quarrying. Just as Iemanjá is to be encountered in the surf and sea (for better, her waters give peace and well-being, soothe cramps, bring fertility and reproductive health to her daughters according to Dona Luciana—or, for worse, should she choose to take her child home to her watery palace), Xangô frequents those places where men cut stones from living rock. Dona Marisa, a daughter of Xangô at the House of Father John, used to pass by such a quarry late at night, walking from the bus stop to her home up on a steep mountainside. She dreaded the walk—an isolated place, no lights, alone, a bad part of town. One night she heard steps behind her, closing in, closer, closer; unable to contain herself, she looked over her shoulder. A few feet behind her was a big, black goat, eyes glowing red. Waves of relief passed over her. Not a mugger, but assuredly not just a goat. It was Xangô's goat, guardian there in Xangô's granite yard.[7] After that it followed Dona Marisa every night that she passed by the quarry.

Dona Luciana's destination on this particular early evening was not a quarry per se (although she referred to it as such) but rather a jumble of granite boulders at the foot of the great granite outcropping that abruptly closes the north end of the beach. I do not know the origin of the boulders; quite possibly they were cut or blasted off to construct the walkway around the outcropping. I don't think they are a natural feature, so in that respect Dona Luciana was correct to seek Xangô there, where men cut stones from living rock. She and Ronaldo were there that evening, a Wednesday (Xangô's day of the week) at the end of September (the 30th is the feast day for St Geronimo, with whom he is associated) to make their annual offering. Kneeling in the sand by a boulder a short distance from the calm water's edge, Dona Luciana arranged the tray while Ronaldo scooped a hole in the sand to shield the candle from the wind. He lit it;

they prayed, they felt Xangô's presence—and were suddenly bowled over by a breaker from out of nowhere. "It was a *prova* (a proof), of Xangó's power, right there in his quarry, and right there in the home of Iemanjá," Dona Luciana concluded. "Ronaldo and I were quite a sight, soaking wet, dressed in white, shivering, riding the bus back home because we would have died of the cold walking! Imagine!"

Thinking back now on Dona Luciana's story reminds me of something I never told her, or anyone. I had been in Rio for over a year, working with Umbanda, living about a mile from the beach at Ipanema. It was one of those nights when I had no session to attend, nothing much to do but read and work on notes and maybe watch one of those fabulous Brazilian soaps before turning in. But I felt restless, unsettled, and so a little before midnight I put on my sandals and shirt and shorts and started on what I thought would be a brisk walk around the block. I got to the end of the block and just kept going. It was as though I was lost in thought, but I wasn't thinking, just feeling, from out of the blue, very much alone in the world. Lost in feelings, oblivious, my feet directed themselves. I was a good way up the broad mosaic sidewalk that follows the beach before I took any notice of where I was—a couple of miles from home. I kept going, past the broad open beach of Ipanema, down to the Devil's Beach, I believe it is called, where I found a hidden spot to sit in the sand and watch the waves roll in. I thought about the songs Dona Luciana and Ronaldo would sing for Iemanjá and then about one they sing to call the cabocla spirit Jurema, a kind of lieutenant of Iemanjá. I liked the song a lot, it talked about Jurema as a mermaid, as a messenger of Iemanjá, and it seemed appropriate, there on the beach, my back toward the city, in the wee hours, enveloped by the sound of low surf and touch of sea breeze, to sing it, over and over (with her harpoon in her hand, with her mermaid's song, she comes here to earth . . . to help the faithful). Perhaps I was dozing off. What happened next I consciously remember only as fragments of images and sensations, tumbling as in a kaleidoscope. But sometimes when I think about it as I sit dozily on some afternoon, in those moments between waking and dreaming, the jumbles fall into place to form something like a coherent memory. The little swells morph into mermaids and then smiling dolphin faces, winking and grinning with silvery sea foam teeth, bobbing up and down, invite me to join them on the undulating edge of salt water and night wind, in a liquid world where one is never alone. And then I was with them, bobbing on the sea, "We all talk dolphin here," one tells me in whistles and clicks, one warm flipper around my shoulder, cradling a scotch in his other, "you'll pick it up in no time."

A wave from nowhere splashed over me, and the water rose over my hips. I stood up. It was nearly four.

CHAPTER 2

The Path

THE BUS

I don't know if there were many other passengers or just a few on the bus that afternoon in 1990; for me the bus was full of emptiness and the anticipation of little more than nothing. My eyes focused on the mirrored inner surfaces of my own sad cocoon; the lively eyes and living flesh that may have surrounded me were just the blurred, fragmented background of a lonely journey. The bus roared and lurched its way toward my apartment in a very nice neighborhood of Rio de Janeiro, but my work and my life were on a path to nowhere, it seemed. I was a few months into more than a year of field research with Umbanda and, despite my efforts, I just could not seem to get off the ground. I had come to Rio with one solid connection, Dona Luciana, the Umbanda priestess I had worked with a few years earlier for a summer, and a plan to expand my research to work with a number of groups representing the diverse range of Umbanda. And now, after tips that led nowhere, introductions that didn't pan out, I had achieved a grand total of—almost nothing. And it was now December; even if I could find centers that would work with me, they wouldn't be doing anything over the holiday month, and then would only hold a session or two in January before breaking for Carnival, and then for Lent. I still had my Umbanda priestess, Dona Luciana, with whom I had worked a few years earlier, and I did find another Umbanda center where the leader warmly welcomed my presence. But, in fact, I was allowed to do nothing more than watch. When I asked questions about what I was seeing or about the history of the place, or about the people who came there, the answer was always "Excuse me, I'm sure I can answer your questions, but first I must check with the *chefe*" (boss). They always provided me with a guide, usually the same very polite, friendly middle-aged woman, but I soon learned my guide was really a minder, there to make sure I didn't poke my nose into the wrong corner—or even the right one, for that matter.[1] My hope was that, if I stuck it out, at some point they would come to trust me, but deep down I knew that path was nothing but a blind alley. In fact, I was just on my way home from that place for the last time, sad and frustrated and more than a little sure of my own worthlessness as an anthropologist and as a person—well, you see, the instrument of ethnographic research is oneself, one's ability to reach out, to listen, to interpret, to connect, and I certainly wasn't doing much connecting and so I couldn't be much of an anthropologist—when somehow a bit of light pierced my gray cocoon—there, off in a bit of woods, was a gate, and on top of it were several clay vessels—bowls, and jars—receptacles for offerings and devotions to the orixás!

It was too late to pull the buzzer to get off; I would have to go all the way back around on the enormous circular route. But maybe, I thought, that circular path at least has a destination; at the end, not a pot of gold, but better, a place to learn and listen, to take in and open out, a place to do the work of ethnography. Or, maybe, it's just another trip down another blind alley.

THE PATH

Winding its way through much of what Umbandistas say about life, cosmos, and personal history is the word *caminho*, which variously refers to road (the usual gloss), street, trail, way, track, or path. In Umbanda parlance, caminho is a metaphor, and to me the word "path" feels closest to its intent in most cases. But sometimes it means more like what we would convey by "way," for instance in "o caminho da luz" the way of light (as in enlightenment and truth and right). Sometimes it has the sense of "trails," as in a line from a song that closes many Umbanda sessions: "*uma estrela no céu, guiou nosso pai; guiai esses filhos caminhos que vai*" (a star in the sky guided our Father; guide these children whatever trails they take). The melody of the song, its happy and affectionate mood, and the fact that it is a leave-taking resonates so well with our own "happy trails, to you." Path, way, trail, road; for simplicity, I will just translate it as "path."

Path is a flexible metaphor, applicable to a whole range of things. Umbanda is itself a path, one of many that my informants esteem as spiritual. Judaism, Islam, Christianity, Hinduism, Buddhism, Spiritism, those are all paths, Ronaldo told me, each valid, each leading, in its own way, for its own place and time, to truth. "My path," he said, "just happens to be Umbanda." The path can be a metaphor of the contents of one's heart and character. Egoism, greed, dishonesty—those put a person on a bad path. The loving heart, the open hand, the humble spirit—the person with those qualities walks the good path. Path is also frequently used to talk about a personal path, that specific constellation of actions, accidents, passions, proclivities, coincidences, triumphs, disasters, joys, and heartbreaks that make up one's unique life. In this usage, path becomes a powerful metaphor indeed. It implies that one is going somewhere; that those seemingly random meanders and twists and turns really follow some kind of cryptic map, if we can just read it. That things happen for a reason. For instance, that little series of missed chances, small successes and larger failures, and providence that led a discouraged and depressed anthropologist to get on a particular bus one particular afternoon and look in a particular direction at just a certain moment and see, through a crack in his gloom, a little path off the side of the road that led to somewhere—on his path.

This chapter tells of the paths of three people deeply involved with Umbanda. That is a very small number. Diana Brown estimated in 1986 that more than ten million Brazilians regularly participate in Umbanda, and millions more do so occasionally. Three can hardly represent ten million, and each of these three is highly unusual in some important ways. One is Dona Luciana, the woman we met in Chapter 1, who practices Umbanda for a small circle of friends in her little apartment in Copacabana. Another is a highly charismatic, dynamic leader of a large and vital Umbanda center; his name is Seu Silva. Both of these are extraordinary, far, far from the norm in many, many ways. And yet, they are exquisitely representative, in much the same way that a gifted poet or artist is representative—not by being average, but by virtue of their ability to dramatically *represent* and give voice to deep cultural and psychic themes and processes. Each represents a major current within Umbanda—Dona Luciana's style of Umbanda is generally known as *Umbanda branca*, (White Umbanda) while that of Seu Silva celebrates the African heritage in Umbanda. As different as they and their versions of Umbanda are, the paths that brought them to Umbanda are perhaps not all that different, and I believe they tell us a lot about the paths of many, many other Umbandistas. The third person whose path I briefly discuss is not Brazilian, not an Umbandista, but perhaps more deeply touched by it than many who are. That would be me.

DONA LUCIANA

The Umbanda priestess who represented the one bright, productive spot in my journey as I rode the bus that afternoon was Dona Luciana, with whom I had started working back in 1986. Dona Luciana at that time was in her late sixties, a petite woman with ivory skin, broad high cheekbones, and straight raven hair that fell thick to the small of her back. Were her skin darker, as it might have been had she spent more time in the sun away from her apartment and the perpetually shaded high rise canyons of Copacabana, she would have looked very much like the mental image I have of the Indian princess Jurema, one of the many spirits that she received during the weekly Umbanda sessions she held in the bedroom of her little Copacabana apartment. Even more striking than her appearance, Dona Luciana had a charm, a playfulness, a fluidity of speech and move- ment, an inventiveness with words and stories, and an intuitive, empathic, and kindly nature that drew the affectionate, admiring attention of a small circle, mostly middle-aged women, but also a handful of younger folks who frequented her weekly sessions. They were drawn to Dona Luciana but, even more, they were drawn by her spirits, an assortment of fascinating characters splendidly enacted by Dona Luciana, who, under different circumstances or perhaps in another lifetime, could easily have been an actor of enormous charisma.

Dona Luciana's path to Umbanda was at once unique and stereotypical. As a young woman and well into middle age, working with the spirits was the last thing that Dona Luciana would have wanted to do. Brought up in a wealthy family, the daughter of Portuguese immigrants, her spiritual upbringing was strictly Catholic. Macumba[2] was a thing of the poor, the uneducated, the working class, and, especially, the black—redolent of ignorance, superstition, even sexual scandal and violence, at least according to the dominant ideology of the times.[3] As a child Dona Luciana attended private schools; as a young woman, she passed *carnaval* not in the street but in exclusive clubs; and as a young mother, her home was in a fine neighborhood, her house kept by servants, expenses budgeted from the earnings of her successful lawyer husband. The world of Macumba was as exotic and distasteful to this younger Dona Luciana as the lives of the poor who did Rio's work and lived in its hillside slums were to the friends and family she lunched with in the chic restaurants. Her path was privileged, materialistic, and thoroughly mundane.

Her path took a sharp turn in the 1960s, a period of tumultuous upheaval in the social and cultural landscape. A coup in 1964 established a military dictatorship that would last for twenty years. The coup essentially was a reaction against a tidal wave of social change threatening the interests of the privileged classes, of which Dona Luciana was certainly a member. A series of increasingly repressive military regimes by and large succeeded in suppressing demands for economic and social justice, but the psychological foundations of middle- and upper-class comfort were shaken. Simultaneously, cultural earthquakes rocked Dona Luciana's world, threatening her ethical and aesthetic values. The root metonym of this upheaval, for her, was the Beatles. Before the Beatles, she told me, everything was different—and much, much better. "They mixed up everything. Boys started looking like girls—you couldn't tell them apart! And look what they did to the music . . . horrible!" Dona Luciana described a snowball effect of loosened morals, drugs, loss of respect for authority, criminality, and on and on. Perhaps Dona Luciana exaggerated for my benefit, knowing as she did where I stood on those matters and enjoying the sport of tweaking me, but her underlying message—that the 1960s represented a massive and threatening social and cultural landslide that affected her in a deeply personal sense—is clear, and entirely consistent with what I heard from other Umbandistas of her social class and generation, and certainly relevant to understanding the rapid growth in middle-class participation in White Umbanda during the 1960s and 1970s.

Beyond the cultural upheaval, the personal ground under Dona Luciana's feet was shaking. Her marriage grew increasingly troubled. In retrospect, Dona Luciana could see signs of trouble early on. Unlike most women of her class and generation, Dona Luciana from an early age aspired to a career. She took courses in business and accounting and saw herself leading an independent life, as a businesswoman or in a profession. But then she fell in love and got married, to a charming and ambitious young lawyer with very traditional notions of gender and family. Dona Luciana became a mother, a housewife; the only business she would administer would be the household. While professing that having and raising her three daughters was a bottomless font of joy and meaning, Dona Luciana would wistfully, rhetorically, ask "What if . . . what if I hadn't given up my career . . . who knows?" (The fact that Dona Luciana fervently supports higher education, careers, and financial independence for young women perhaps answers the question.) Giving up her aspirations and taking up the routines of domestic life could certainly put strains on a person like Dona Luciana and strains on a marriage, but compounding matters, over the years Dona Luciana's husband grew more controlling, more possessive, more jealous. A case in point, Dona Luciana, from an early age, loved music. She was trained in piano, and voice. Within the domestic confines, she found an enormous outlet in her playing, until, one day, men hired by her husband came and took the piano away. The piano, it seems, took up too much space.

The words Dona Luciana used to describe this period in her life were *angústia*, *desgosto*, *decepcões*, and *dor* (anguish, disgust, disappointments, and pain). Nearly thirty years later she still talked about it, occasionally; when she did, I could hear the tone of complaint in her voice, see the confusion and hurt still in her eyes. The picture Dona Luciana's words painted was one of depression and desperation. Neither medicine nor friends nor family could put her back on her feet. Dona Luciana was at the *fim do caminho* (the end of the road).

Then a friend talked her into going to an Umbanda session. Dona Luciana had no desire to go—the stereotype of Macumba frightened and revolted her—but her depression and anguish left her little will to resist. She went.

While the intensity of suffering that led Dona Luciana to the Umbanda center that night may have been unusual—the fact is that most people come to Umbanda, at least initially, because they are having problems. The spirits offer guidance, protection, healing, hope. The sufferer can lay out her troubles to the old slave, or the Indian, or the Gypsy, whatever the spirit; the spirit listens and probes, untwists the knots, sees underneath the appearances to the spiritual roots of the trouble. Beyond advice, the spirit often prescribes concrete action: make an offering to Iemanjá, the sea goddess, perhaps seven roses at the water's edge. Or: bring to the next session seven white candles, one spool each of red, black, and white thread, a half-kilo of raw sugar, a bottle of honey, and a medium unglazed clay bowl, and the Gypsy will do a "work" to make your husband sweet on you again, and tie him with threads of love and passion to his home. Or go to the forest and light a candle and set out a bottle of muscatel and a corncob pipe full of rough tobacco for the old slave spirit Father John to give you strength and settle your jangled nerves. These conversations between spirit and sufferer may be deep, intense, and desperately important, but there is little obvious drama; one sees, for example, a young woman seated on a little white stool in front of a middle-aged man dressed in white, hunched over and smoking a pipe—an old slave spirit—their faces close together. They talk in low voices, calmly; he takes her hands in his, then snaps his fingers above her head and down the length of her body, hugs her, right chest and left, and she walks away as a worried looking middle-aged man comes to sit on the stool she just vacated. The spirit may counsel five or ten or even more troubled people in a night's work; and it is almost always like this, quiet, essentially private, and not at all dramatic.

Sometimes, though, the encounter can be violently dramatic. This is most often the case when the person is suffering extremes of agitation or depression, as Dona Luciana was. A person in these conditions is said to be afflicted by negative spirits. She might have a malevolent spirit *encostado*—leaning on her, tormenting her, distorting her perceptions and judgments, robbing her energy, placing obstacles in her path, afflicting her heart with rage or sadness or anxiety. When a person in this desperate condition is brought to an Umbanda center, she may spontaneously fall into a violent trance, jerking, flailing, falling backwards as the malevolent spirit takes over. This is serious business. When it occurs, the personnel of the center spring into action. The patient—I'll use that word, because it is a crisis, and the person is seen as a patient; I have heard the response of the center personnel likened to the actions of an emergency room team—is surrounded by mediums and restrained to avoid injury until the convulsions pass. At this point the patient may be sobbing, or even cursing and screaming, possessed by the bad spirit or spirits. One or more of the mediums address the spirit, imploring it to identify itself, alternatively cajoling and demanding that it leave the patient alone, advising it to seek the light, and sending it away, hopefully for good. The patient returns to herself, typically looking a bit bewildered and somewhat spent, but no longer agitated. The crisis is past, the tension is gone, the effect is cathartic, and sometimes that is all that is needed. But oftentimes it is not; unfortunately, the patient in many cases suffers recurring attacks. In the latter case, the patient may be diagnosed as being unusually susceptible to spirits, the only cure being to learn to control that sensitivity and turn it to the good—to become, that is, a medium.

Dona Luciana came to the Umbanda center that night deeply, deeply troubled. She did not, however, fall into the convulsions of involuntary trance. Nor were her problems dealt with in quiet consultation with an old slave or an Indian. Her path took a dramatically different turn— unprecedented, actually.

THE HOUSE OF FATHER JOHN

During my first trip to Brazil I had met Dona Luciana, and that had been very productive and I continued to work with her. Early on during my second trip (1990) I was introduced to another small Umbanda center, the House of Saint Benedict, this one headed by a woman in her eighties who seemed at least twenty years younger. This relationship, too, was productive. My anxieties though stemmed mainly from the fact that both Dona Luciana's little group and the House of Saint Benedict were not representative of the whole spectrum of Umbanda and Umbanda participants. Most Umbandistas are working class or lower class and, while many would be considered *brancos* (whites), most are not. In many Umbanda centers, the connection to Afro-Brazilian origins is palpable, in the drumming that summons the spirits, the emphasis on the orixás, the African gods, and in the blood sacrifices—chickens mainly, but also guinea fowl, sheep, goats, even bulls—to the various deities. But Dona Luciana, while not herself wealthy, was hardly a member of the "popular" classes, as the working and lower classes are called in Latin America, and neither was Dona Linda, the leader at the House of Saint Benedict. Dona Linda's deceased husband, in fact, had been a successful businessman (and Umbanda leader) and among the mediums who worked with her and the persons who sought the aid of their spirits were wives of military officers and other members of the professional middle class. And the Umbanda they practiced carried little hint at all of African traditions. No drumming, no sacrifice; instead, the rituals and beliefs were more on the *Kardecismo* path, a form of spiritualism imported from France and permeated with esoteric doctrines of karma, vibrations, levels of spiritual evolution, and references to ancient Egypt and Atlantis. This was all fascinating, but to get the full picture of Umbanda, to get some sociological insight into why some Umbanda takes the form of White Umbanda, as at the House of Saint Benedict, and why other Umbanda centers embrace African traditions, in order to discuss Umbanda within the contexts of its participants, when those contexts range from the well-off to the poor and across the spectrum of racial identity, for that, I needed another site. Looking out that window, seeing those clay jars on top of the gate, I dared hope: Perhaps this would be it?

I would get back on that bus. When it rounded the bend just before where I had seen the gate with the little clay jars and bowls, I got off. I didn't notice the little buzzer so I hauled back my fist to pound hard on the thick metal door at the gate. At that moment the door opened and a smiling, robust young man greeted me. I introduced myself and expressed my interest in Umbanda. He warmly invited me to return that evening to the Spiritual Center of Father John, named after an old slave who died on that very spot and whose spirit now guides the place—they would be having a *gira*, a dance to celebrate the orixás, and then a session for people to consult with the spirits. "Don't miss it!"

A LECTURE IN PORTUGUESE CLASS

I could say that I stepped on the path that led me to Umbanda by chance, but Umbandistas by and large are skeptical of coincidence, at least in the large things in life. Things happen for a reason. What may appear to be random events are really clues to an underlying design; pitfalls and stumbles and inexplicable good fortune or bad appear, especially in hindsight, as signs leading the person toward her path. But my path to and through Umbanda would certainly seem haphazard enough—or, alternatively, improbable enough as to indicate the work of unseen forces, at least to Umbanda eyes.

I first heard about Umbanda while taking a Portuguese course as a senior in college. I was in the course because I was double majoring in Anthropology and Spanish, and I could forego two upper division litera- ture courses by taking a year of Portuguese. My instructor, a Fulbright scholar, had recently returned from a year in Brazil. Every few weeks Professor Dow would give a presentation on some aspect of Brazilian cul- ture. One such presentation concerned the popular religions in Brazil. As I recall (this was twenty-five years ago, and memory does have a life of its own), she talked about the folk Catholicism of rural people, who would make pilgrimages to a remote shrine in the backlands, making good on a promise to a saint who cured their illness or found their lost cattle. There was the esoteric Spiritualism (referred to as espiritismo or kardecismo) imported from France in the nineteenth century, which featured séances around a table with mediums channeling the spirits of scholars, artists, physicians, and statesmen. I was deeply moved by her account of the tra- ditional Afro-Brazilian Candomblé,[4] for its rich mythology and awesome ritual, but even more by the fact that slaves and their descendents kept these traditions alive—and in many ways, the traditions kept those people alive—for hundreds of years of captivity and oppression. The professor's discussion of Macumba with its spells and "black magic" and her pictures of garish statuettes representing such spirits as Zé Pelintra, depicted as a goateed bohemian type dressed in a white linen suit, panama hat, bare- foot, smoking a cigar and cradling a bottle of cachaça in the crook of his arm, and Maria Padilha, crimson skinned, buxom and topless, the very picture of deliciously transgressive sexuality, really grabbed my imagina- tion. It was an hour of utter fascination for me.

Coincidentally or not, at that moment I was looking for inspiration or, at least, a topic for my senior thesis. I started the semester thinking I would write about the system of regional markets in Oaxaca, Mexico, but, as I read more and more, I realized that economic anthropology was not a good fit for me. My real interests were symbolism, religion, and tradition, not as abstractions or systems, but as these come alive in people's creative, imaginative ways of living, both at the moment and through the crucible of history. Candomblé and Macumba seemed to be incredibly rich sites to look at. At the library, I soon decided that a comparison of Candomblé and Umbanda—the latter an enormously popular and important religion based on Afro-Brazilian roots that had sprung up in the early decades of the twentieth century in Rio de Janeiro—would allow me to explore the relationship between religious form and social/historical contexts. So I read and read and, near the end of the spring term, I wrote. The reading laid a foundation for infinitely more reading on Afro-Brazilian religion; the writing was the beginning of almost everything I have written since. Pure coincidence, no doubt.

DONA LUCIANA GOES TO UMBANDA

So what happened that first night that Dona Luciana stepped foot in an Umbanda center? She was possessed, all right, but not in a violent, convulsive crisis, and not by evil spirits. It was all very calm. First came the spirit of the Indian named Mata Virgem. He introduced himself, and then "opened the way" for a succession of others—an old slave named Gerônimo, a child spirit who went by Pedrinho (Little Peter), another old slave, a Chinese man, a lady of the evening, and a little Indian girl, among others. Whereas it often takes months, or longer, of training for a medium to reach the point where her spirits are articulate and controlled, and even longer to develop an extensive retinue, Dona Luciana reported that it was as if she were born for this, already "developed," as one describes an experienced medium.

Perhaps she was. Dona Luciana reports that when she was very young, she was often visited at night by an elderly Chinese gentleman with long black hair tied in a braid and dressed in silk robes who would watch over her, smiling slightly, illuminated perhaps by the moonlight or perhaps by a spiritual light from within. His presence made her feel warm and happy and not alone. By day she was visited by other friends no one else could see—a little black boy, an Indian girl, even some children who spoke some other language besides Portuguese. Looking back from the perspective of Umbanda, she realized that these were not just the imaginary friends of a lonely child. They were spirits.

One of these was particularly salient. He was a boy with wavy, chestnut hair and blue eyes, dressed in a white robe and sandals, appearing to be about Dona Luciana's age at the time, around seven. One day he appeared outside the open door of the classroom, beckoning to Luciana to come and play. Luciana made the sign to the nun to be excused to go to the bathroom. Once out of the room, she chased the boy up the hallway and out the back door. Their game of hide and seek led finally to the chapel. Dona Luciana looked and looked, but couldn't find the boy. Tired, she lay down by the altar and slept and slept until evening when the nuns, who had searched up and down and worried themselves sick, came to the chapel for evening prayers. There they found Luciana. They woke her; she opened her eyes, and the first thing she saw was a painting of Christ as a young boy, with Mary—lo and behold, the spitting image of her little friend! Dona Luciana won't say that it really was Jesus, but she does say that in her child's mind at the time it was Jesus, and she takes the incident as yet another sign to her of her true path.

But just as a child's imagination gives way to banal realities of grown up life, so Luciana's spirits receded far, far back until, like the old Chinese gentleman and the Indian girl, they would meet her on the path that night in the 1960s.

SEU SILVA

Even if I had known where I was going that afternoon, I could not have found a better place to further my research than the House of Father John. I felt it immediately. It certainly represented the most "African" traditions in Umbanda. By the gate as I entered that evening was a large clay bowl half full of manioc flour, an onion cut in quarters, the head, wings, and feet of a chicken, its blood spotting the surrounding ground, its white feathers and the yellow manioc splashed with the bright yellow-orange of palm oil—an offering to Exu, the intermediary between the orixás and us, guardian of the crossroads, the trickster who opens our paths or closes them. Inside the gate, along the path to the terreiro, were shrines to various orixás—a little house for Omolu, the god of sickness and healing; a boulder with an iron point imbedded for Xangô, the god of thunder and justice and master of stoneworking; and another house for Oxalá, the sky god and creator of mankind whose drunken mishaps in shaping the clay of life made us crippled and ugly and flawed in body and mind. Inside, three drums stood against the wall. Bare feet walked on the hard-packed earth floor.

I would meet some wealthy people there, and a number of the mediums as well as visitors were comfortably middle class, but the well-off were in the minority. More numerous were folks who lived in the favelas, the mountainside slums perched above the wealthy neighborhoods, and others from the far-flung, working-class suburbs. Some had jobs as laborers or clerks, some did odd jobs, a few sold cheap jewelry or toys, cigarette lighters, and tools or questionable "imported" whiskey or underwear from the stands that jammed the sidewalks of Copacabana and downtown. Some had no jobs at all. And, at the opposite end of the socioeconomic spectrum, were a wealthy few who drank their lives from the rich cream floating atop the thin, thin milk that barely sustains the masses.

Seu Silva,[5] the leader and founder of the House of Father John, was like Dona Luciana only in the sense of possessing an enormous charisma, but his was of a very different flavor. Seu Silva was a robust, earthy man, a low mountain of flesh and thick bone. Where Dona Luciana's spirits seemed almost amplifications of her own mixture of elegance, playfulness, sentimentality, and storytelling, Seu Silva's seemed to burst from a Rabelaisian dream, all passion, earth, and sweat—a fleshy, rollicking, sensuous spirituality. At the House of Father John there was the charm of the grotesque, the carnivalesque, that had intrigued me about Macumba during that lecture years before—and, indeed, the folks at the House of Father John jokingly and with some pride referred to themselves and to me as *macumbeiros*, practitioners of Macumba, laughing in the face of the prejudice implied by the word.

Seu Silva's path took a sudden turn toward Umbanda not long after Dona Luciana's first experience. It seemed that his life was going rather well, at least on the surface. He had a good job, an apartment, a wife, a normal, materialistic, everyday life. But something was not quite right. Something was disturbing his sleep, his thoughts, his emotions. Perhaps just the stress of his job, nothing more, he told himself. Then very late one night he found himself suddenly and frighteningly awake, bare-chested, sitting on a grave in a cemetery miles from home. Another night he awoke knee deep in the surf, again shirtless, again miles from home. And on other occasions, less frightening, his wife would find him in the wee hours sitting hunched over on the floor of their apartment, muttering in a kind of pidgin Portuguese.

Seu Silva sought professional help, to no avail. Eventually a friend convinced him to go with him to see a man who worked with spirits. As I imagine the scene that night, based on what he told me, Seu Silva, empty of hope and full of despair, sat on a little stool opposite this man, who at that moment was possessed by the spirit of an old slave. Puffing his pipe, looking into Seu Silva's eyes, feeling his forehead and heart, asking some questions, listening and listening, smoking and smoking, pondering and searching, the old slave untangled the web. It had been the old slave Joaquim, muttering pidgin Portuguese in the wee hours in the apartment. It was the exu Tranca Rua who marched him to the graveyard and into the surf where the sea goddess Iemanjá lives. The old slave passed his hands over Seu Silva, and Seu Silva fell into a trance, possessed by Joaquim. When Seu Silva came to, he received the diagnosis: the spirits are calling you to serve them, as a medium. Take that path—or dance.[6]

Seu Silva would not hear of it. To quit his job, leave behind a regular life, one that once had been a good one, spend his days and nights

receiving spirits and making offerings, giving his life over to the orixás—
no. How would he live?

A TRIP TO BRAZIL

When I first went to Brazil I had no intention of studying Umbanda,
although I had read quite a bit about it in researching my senior thesis.
I knew that it had begun in the early twentieth century, when practitioners of Afro-Brazilian religion incorporated some ideas, language, and
practices from French Spiritualism. I knew that it had been very much
affected by the stigma attached to Afro-Brazilian religions and that, at least
in the variety known as White Umbanda, almost anything associated with
Africa—drumming and sacrifice, particularly—had been banished, along
with the use of alcohol during ritual, exuberant all-night celebrations,
and anything else that might offend bourgeois sensibilities. Its founders
aspired to middle-class respectability, embracing the dominant ideology
that disparaged Afro-Brazilian culture as antithetical to order and progress
and modern civilization. I knew that much of its self-published literature
consisted of arcane, sometimes impenetrable doctrine—spiritual phalan-
ges, levels, hierarchies, vibrations, references to Atlantis and Rosicrucians,
alchemy and karma. There were spirits of Indians, sometimes garbed in
headdresses straight out of Hollywood or cigar-store iconography; old
slaves presented as broad caricatures, Brazilian versions of Uncle Tom,
Uncle Remus, or Aunt Jemima. A little silly and stilted, and certainly
suspect ideologically. Or so my reading led me to believe. What I wanted
to study was Candomblé, the traditional Afro-Brazilian religion, rich in
mythology, authentic in ritual, a living testament to resistance and survival through centuries of oppression of African peoples in Brazil. And I
planned to study it in Salvador, the capital of Bahia, the center of authentic Afro-Brazilian culture.

But my path didn't exactly lead where I wanted to go; from an
Umbanda perspective, perhaps it was never meant to. I arrived in Rio,
planning to spend a few days there before flying up to Salvador. I went to

the National Museum to meet with the anthropologist Gilberto Velho, director of graduate studies in anthropology at the Federal University in Rio. He didn't think much of my going to Salvador. The place was crawling with anthropologists, he warned; besides, "so much work has been done there, how about looking at Rio? You'll find interesting things here. At least stay a week or so and read the dissertations our students have written." With polite insincerity, I said I would consider it. He sent me off to see another anthropologist, Peter Fry, who told me much the same thing. Again I promised to consider it. I did not cancel my ticket to Salvador.

I did start in on the dissertations though. The first one was superb[7]—I decided to delay my trip a few days. Besides, I was really enjoying Rio, and a friend had given me the number of a friend who had an aunt who did Umbanda. Why not at least get a taste? I called the number, using my best Portuguese, which apparently was not very good at all at that point. The lady who answered hung up on me. I called again. Click. The third time I managed to blurt out an intelligible plea not to hang up. It was my friend's friend's mother. She invited me to drop by; her daughter would be home the next afternoon. I could explain my business to her. I did, and the next evening she took me to Dona Luciana's.

I never left Rio. Salvador, apparently, was not on my path.

THE BIG EYE

Dona Luciana may have lost her marriage, but she found a life that long-ago night at the Umbanda center. She proved to be, as she put it, a born medium. Whereas most beginners struggle at times to go into trance and only gradually develop a "crown" of several spirits over many months or years, this all came easily and rapidly to Dona Luciana. There were, to just name a few, Mata Virgem the Indian; Gerônimo, the slave; Jurema, an Indian princess who, as we shall see, was not an Indian at all and who sang with the trained voice of an opera singer; a Spanish Crusader, Senhor Hernán de la Arena; and Mari-Carmen, a flamenco dancer who played castanets and wore a yellow rose in her hair. I have met them all (years later, of course). All were acclaimed for their efficacy, but, perhaps equally important, each represented a dramatic, compelling, complex character. Dona Luciana's spirits were good theater. She, or they, drew a crowd.

While humility and dedication to the mission of spiritual charity are core values in Umbanda, the fact is that egoism, jealousy, and competition are as much a part of the dynamics of Umbanda centers as they are of any organization. Underneath the rhetoric of charity and cooperation, latent competitive strains are apparent. As the Brazilian anthropologist Yvonne Velho demonstrated in her classic ethnographic study, these latent strains can burst forth in overt, schismatic conflict.[8] The anthropologist George Foster wrote long ago about the "image of limited good," the attitude he found in closed, corporate, peasant communities that the success of the individual comes at the expense of others. While there may not be much in the way of material goods at stake in an Umbanda center, there is a kind of economy of prestige and power, and these are limited (and intertwined), which generates both a formal and informal hierarchy. Formally, place is marked by offices, such as *chefe do terreiro* (boss of the terreiro) or *mãe de santo* (mother of saint; the male equivalent is *pai de santo*, father of saint), *mãe pequena* (little mother, a second-in-command), *presidente* (responsible for secular, business affairs), and so forth. Informally, it is marked by (and largely achieved through) the popularity and prestige of mediums' spirit entities, which usually, in a rough way, correspond to length of experience. As long as participants accept their place in the hierarchy, as long as they do not openly covet higher office or higher prestige, or (inadvertently or otherwise) threaten the status quo with displays of exceptional talent or energy, a tenuous peace holds over this economy of limited good. But people are people, and people are prone to envy or, in that wonderfully apt Brazilian metaphor, for envy *olho grande* "big eye."

One evening, sometime after becoming a regular medium at that Umbanda center where we last saw Dona Luciana, the spirit Jurema visited. Her voice sailed forth from Dona Luciana's mouth, wordlessly echoing the images evoked by the song telling of Jurema as a mermaid, guiding sailors across stormy seas. Dona Luciana's body took a seat on a low stool, knees, ankles, and feet together, knees slightly bent, suggesting the mermaid's tail, while she let down her hair to flow over one shoulder.[9] Having seen this many times years later, I can imagine she was the center of everyone's attention. Suddenly, the leader of the center stormed up, yanked Dona Luciana to her feet, and accused her of being a showoff and a fraud. He demanded that Dona Luciana demonstrate her remorse, humility, and submission by cutting her hair—something that Jurema had forbidden her to do.

"There it is," Dona Luciana told me, "big eye. He had envy for me, he felt threatened, but it wasn't me trying to take his place or put myself above anyone. I was just carrying out my spiritual mission, with all humility. Big eye. It's sad, isn't it?"

Dona Luciana left that place that night and never went back. Sometime later, something very similar happened at another place. But in the latter incident, Jurema instructed a woman there to give a message to Dona Luciana. Jurema's message was that Dona Luciana speak to a woman named Vera. Vera, who Dona Luciana barely knew, took Dona Luciana that night to yet another Umbanda center. The leader there told Dona Luciana that she couldn't work in his center or anyone else's: these incidents were a sign from the orixás that her true path was to become a mãe de santo, a priestess, presiding over her own center. He would have his nephew initiate and ordain her, and then she would be on her own.

FATHER JOHN GOES FOR A WALK

Seu Silva was in a fix. One might even say his faith was being tested, and not for the first time. Several years back, when he had suffered his crisis, that old slave had told him that his only chance was to devote himself to the orixás, to become their instrument, their medium. He resisted that advice. How would he live without a job? Or, he *would* have resisted, but his situation was really untenable. He couldn't go on. He gave himself over to the orixás. And somehow, things worked out. A doctor affirmed that he was medically unfit for work. His disability entitled him to some money. His spirits were formidable, real problem solvers. They soon drew a crowd. Although Umbandistas make a point of not charging for their work with spirits, grateful clients are known to help out materially. They helped Seu Silva. He got by. Seu Silva had walked on the edge of an abyss; the orixás did not let him fall.

But on this day his path once again wound round the edge of a cliff. Earlier that day he had been in his apartment with a few friends who shared in his work with spirits. Perhaps they had been preparing for one of their weekly sessions, when numerous people—far too numerous for his neighbors' comfort—would line up to consult with his spirits, oftentimes into the late hours. In any event, Seu Silva suddenly went into a trance, possessed by the spirit of an old slave, Father John. Father John announced they were going to take a walk. They walked and walked, Father John smoking his pipe, his eyes looking about as though for familiar landmarks in the now thoroughly urbanized geography. Finally they arrived in a wooded spot, at the foot of a steep, steep hill. Father John knelt down and scratched a little hole in the dirt. "This is it. This is where I planted my root from Africa, long, long ago. You tell Seu Silva to build my house right here." Father John's tone and bearing indicated this was an order.

When Seu Silva came to himself and heard of this, it filled him with worry. He couldn't carry out this obligation. He had no money to buy the land; even if he could somehow get the land, how in the world could he build an Umbanda center? Who would design it? Who would build it? Who would pay for it? He couldn't do this. But he could not *not* do it either. The spirits had saved him, and they could as easily destroy him. And would. The spirits that work through Seu Silva are generous, kind, often funny, but there is something truly serious, an aura of danger, about them. Dealing with them, as they say, is no joke.

Seu Silva and the spirits that speak through him often point out that the path of truth is a hard one, but not to despair: the orixás never give us more than we can take; if we break, it's our fault for giving in to our doubts. Surely at this moment doubt gnawed at Seu Silva's insides, but he kept on his path. The story got out among those who had benefited from the works of Seu Silva's spirits. Some of them had money, some had connections, some had skills. Inquiries were made, money collected; the land was secured, plans were drawn, work was done, and the house of Father John was built on the spot where, they say, centuries ago an old man who had once been a powerful warrior and sorcerer in Africa before he was sold into slavery, had, in his last moment on earth, planted the root from which Seu Silva's Umbanda now grows.

CHURCH

What grabbed my imagination and held it tight that afternoon many years ago in my Portuguese class was not so much the theoretical significance of those religions, nor their theological characteristics, as it was their sheer theatricality. The spectacular costumes and dancing of the Candomblé, when the deities themselves descend into the bodies of the dancers and make themselves present—just the still images of the slides moved me. And these conversations between spirits and folks seeking their protection and healing—the dramas and tragedies of everyday life worked over by these mediums, portraying or receiving the spirits of old slaves and Indian princesses—what fascinating performances those must be. And those spells and charms and amulets and midnight offerings at the crossroads to attract love or money, to ward off evil eye and envy, to thwart enemies—it all seemed so dramatic, so theatrical, so *magical*. It sparkled.

This all, of course, had enormous theoretical significance and appeal. Take the vitality of the Candomblé, surviving through centuries of repression and stigma, and then, in the last decades of the twentieth century, becoming a treasured symbol of Brazilian cultural identity and an icon of African Diaspora culture and politics. Power, resistance, hegemony, identity: all central theoretical concerns in anthropology and history. Or the conversations of spirits and sufferers—these speak to issues in medical and psychological anthropology, as well as the anthropology of performance. And the spells and charms and evil eye—what a field upon which to turn the theoretical lenses of a semiotic or symbolic anthropology, to interpret these not only as folklore but within the lives of everyday people! I felt this theoretical appeal right from the start, and I have researched and written and lectured on these issues and more over the years.

I certainly didn't realize it at the time and perhaps even repressed it, but I think now there was a deeply personal, theological appeal as well. Or perhaps "spiritual" is a better word than theological, because theology denotes a system of beliefs, of propositions about the cosmos, of proscriptions and prescriptions as to how one lives, none of which I find very attractive; whereas the term spirit connotes a freedom and mystery and effervescence and beyond-word-ness that I do find compelling. But at that time I kept that all locked up in my attic, with those other childhood things I had outgrown. I was a scientist or, rather, a social scientist, whatever in the world that could mean in this postmodern day and age. Religion or spirituality were things in the world, products of the mind, symptoms of the times, social constructions, culturally produced scripts, or (why not?) illusions—more than worthy of study and analysis, unworthy of belief or passion. As a social scientist, I could look at religion as something that people do, explainable like the eye-shaped spots on a certain species of butterfly that scare away predators. Granted, the causes may be multiple and some more convincing than others (religion offers an explanation of the universe, emotional comfort, opium for the masses, that sort of thing), but they must be there and my task would be to dig them out. Belief was simply out of the question.

And yet there was something about all of this that tickled and teased at a spirituality I had abandoned as a child. When I was very young I truly enjoyed church, Sunday School, and Bible stories. Not out of any moral conviction, certainly not out of any consuming devotion to God—indeed, by the time I was nine or ten his behavior in these stories and Sunday School book depictions struck me as those of a spoiled and brutal old tyrant. Our Father appeared to me an overgrown, bearded, white-haired, mean-looking old man. But I loved so many of the stories, loved suspending disbelief as the seas parted before Moses or the few loaves and fishes fed the multitude (a word never heard outside of church, which was a part of it too—the language, I loved the mysterious language) or Jonah passed an adventure in the belly of a whale. The crazy physics didn't bother me, nor did these "miracles" impress me as some kind of proof of God's power. But they did give me a very early and deep feeling of an important part of what I would now call spirituality—the mind carried free on currents of images, living for the moment in the lines of a poem or the words of a storyteller. And there was more spirit, more enchantment, outside of church. I was sort of a little animist; the rocks and trees were alive and sentient, to say nothing of the animals, whose thoughts, if I could not read them exactly, I could certainly imagine. I lived for a while as a child in an enchanted world, but I soon enough left that behind. I became concerned with truth—either something was true, or not, and of course physics and biology won hands down over long-ago Jewish raconteurs (at twelve I was a little too rigid to entertain such notions as "metaphorical truth"). I became disgusted with the church that had once been a playhouse for my spiritual imagination as I became acutely and somewhat self-righteously indignant over the hypocrisy at every turn. A gospel of peace, pews full of supporters of the Vietnam War; fine talk of Brotherhood on Sunday, racist jokes the whole week long. Not very many of the camels in these pews were going to make it through the eye of that needle, I remember chortling to myself during one sermon. And though I managed to retain a bit of my old animism in the face of my science, it was really more metaphorical than actual, as in the ecological view of all life as connected.

I grew up, but apparently hadn't quite killed off the enchanted child within. Unknown to me that afternoon as I took in Professor Dow's slides and stories about Brazilian popular religions, I had gotten a glimpse of that child skipping up ahead on the path.

DONA LUCIANA'S BIG UMBANDA CENTER

As with Seu Silva, the spirits had decreed that Dona Luciana must open her own Umbanda center. No other path was open. She, too, felt overwhelmed by the obstacles she imagined in front of her. Running an Umbanda center involves a tremendous amount of work. There are bills to pay, maintenance, supervising the mediums, leading the sessions, setting policies, training and initiating new mediums—all on top of continuing the work of receiving spirits and keeping up one's obligations to them. And before all that begins, there is the problem of finding a suitable place—a building with at least one large room for public ceremonies, big enough for the mediums to dance and hold consultations, with seating for the dozens of visitors who could be expected to seek the spirits' help. Plus a room or rooms for the mediums to change, a room where those undergoing initiations and other rituals involving seclusion could be lodged, and, ideally, space for a small office and a kitchen. Needless to say, a suitable place is not likely to come cheap. But that was the path the spirits set before her; their wish, her command.

Diana Brown, who researched in Rio in the late 1960s, observed that most of the leaders of Umbanda centers, at least the ones she worked with, came from more privileged economic circumstances than their followers. Both Seu Silva's and Dona Luciana's experiences with opening an Umbanda center suggest why that was so: it requires significant economic resources. In Seu Silva's case, these came largely from the connections he had built up over several years working with the spirits. He was not himself wealthy. There were clients who felt very deeply that they owed him—or his spirits—for their health or good fortune, the life of a loved one, a love, spiritual tranquility, or even for their very lives. Nor was Dona Luciana personally wealthy. But her family had means. A favorite son-in-law, not himself an Umbandista, became an important sponsor, and soon Dona Luciana had set up her center in a grand old house where, before long, she was holding sessions twice a week, supervising thirty-five mediums, putting on elaborate public celebrations honoring the orixás and the spirits, and, in general, running a thriving Umbanda center.

But unlike the House of Father John, Dona Luciana's Umbanda center would only last a few years. The immediate cause of its closing was apparently a business decision. The owners of the mansion decided to refurbish the place and put it on the market as a multimillionaire's dream home. Given the times (the 1970s, when Brazil's "economic miracle," a foray into devil take the hindmost, savage capitalism, was producing enormous wealth at the top and stagnant or declining standards of living at the bottom) and the location (one of Rio's best neighborhoods) the property was considered far too valuable to waste on spiritual pursuits. Maybe there was more to the story, maybe the stress of running it all was too much, maybe there was a schism, maybe, but Dona Luciana didn't mention anything like that. So on the day of the child spirits, celebrated on the feast day for the Catholic child martyrs Cosmas and Damian, Dona Luciana threw one last grand celebration and closed her center. After that, she would practice her Umbanda in her little apartment, supervising a few mediums, working the spirits for a dozen or so mostly middle-aged, mostly middle-class, mostly women visitors, most of whom were acquaintances of several years.

Did she miss her big center? Of course, in some ways yes, in some ways no—an awful lot of work and responsibility, she didn't miss that—but, in any event, it didn't matter. That was her path, and, for their reasons, which we might not understand, that is where the spirits wanted her to be.

BAD DEBT

The paths taken by Dona Luciana and Seu Silva are unusual at least in one important respect: most people who become involved in Umbanda do not become leaders of Umbanda centers. Indeed most people who attend Umbanda sessions are there to get help from the spirits, although through this intervention many develop a sense of obligation toward the spirits and will therefore attend annual celebrations honoring the child spirits, or the old slaves, the Indians, or various African deities. They are also likely to make occasional offerings to particular spirits, often out of gratitude for aid rendered but quite often also as part of an ongoing, deeply personal relationship with a spirit seen as one's special protector or guide.

From that large number of occasional participants—and they number in the millions—a much smaller set choose to actively serve the spirits as mediums. Choose, or rather, are *chosen*. Like Dona Luciana and Seu Silva, most mediums report getting involved in Umbanda as a consequence of personal crisis, usually physical illness or emotional distress, a series of bad breaks or, frequently, all of the above. These eventually get diagnosed as signs that the spiritual powers that be have chosen the person and that the only lasting cure is to serve the spirits. Mediums often report initial resistance to this calling, citing the commitment of time and energy, negative reactions from spouses and family or friends, embarrassment, pride, contradictions with their own commitments to conventional Catholicism, materialism or even atheism, among other factors. But, as we saw with Seu Silva, resistance is futile; things just get worse, and, eventually, the individual takes up the path. The details vary from person to person, but for most, the narrative follows the same basic structure.

While the spirits are generous with their help, reciprocity is expected. Often it is little more than a token gift. A frequent visitor to Dona Luciana's spirits brings a ropey hank of black tobacco for the old slave Father Gerônimo and a handful of cigars for the Indian warrior Mata Virgem. Between mediums and their spirits the reciprocity is much greater and obligatory. The debt is large, unpayable even. How can one ever repay the spirits for saving one's health, sanity, for guiding one on a good path through the darkness of this world and beyond? The spirits save, and the medium, in turn, serves.

Choosing to take the path that one has been chosen for is a serious decision. It involves a lifelong obligation to follow the path. But people are people, and people stray. Mediums will miss sessions—too tired from work, too much going on at home, other reasons. The spirits are lenient, up to a point, but too much slacking leads to consequences, reminders from above that promises are to be kept. A sudden illness, backaches, job loss, getting robbed, nearly capsizing in a storm at sea—I have heard all of these and many other misfortunes interpreted as reminders from the spirits of obligations not kept. In these stories, the person eventually gets the message and gets back on the path.

But not always. There was a medium, Joana, who was a regular at Dona Luciana's sessions in 1990 and 1991. Dona Luciana had trained and initiated her. I noted though that by 1993 Joana didn't come around anymore, and I asked Dona Luciana about her. Joana, it seemed, had gotten very busy. She worked in the daytime, took care of her family and home in the evenings, and besides had enrolled in law school at night. She missed more and more sessions, and finally quit coming altogether. Dona Luciana warned her, but she didn't listen. Joana completed her law degree, but couldn't find legal work. Her husband lost his job, something that happened to lots and lots of middle-class Brazilians at the time. Her son broke his leg in several places in a car accident. Promises, it seems, are meant to be kept.

A PROFESSOR'S QUESTION

How is it that Umbanda has attracted millions of followers, from all walks of life? One of my professors in graduate school, impatient with my meanders into performance and symbolism, the look and feel and poetry of ritual, and the role of spirits in individual lives, urged on me that *that* was *the* sociologically important question raised by Umbanda. It *is* an important question, and though my concern is much more with those experiential, phenomenological, and interpretive questions that my professor found so beside the point, it seems that the metaphor of the path actually sheds some light on his question.

First, it is a fact that our life paths are prone to some rocky stretches. With Seu Silva we saw that those rough patches can take a form that we (and they) could classify as severe emotional or mental disturbance. While Dona Luciana did not report episodes of coming to in a graveyard or in the surf under the moonlight, the breakup of her marriage clearly precipitated a period of intense emotional pain, which I could hear in her voice and see in her face as she discussed it a quarter century later. People lose jobs they can't afford to lose, marriages break up, people get acutely ill or chronically disabled, loved ones die, alcohol and drugs take hold of someone's body and soul, life for any number of reasons becomes an inferno or a vale of tears. These things happen in all social classes, but more often and often more devastatingly to those at the bottom, which is a very large number in Brazil. And then are the smaller crises of every-day life. Small crisis or large, Umbanda offers a supportive environment, spirits who listen and offer good advice, testimonials of diseases cured, addictions licked, battles won. Equally important, perhaps, there is com-fort and some confidence and courage in imagining that a wise old slave and a brave warrior is there on one's dark path.

Second, Umbanda does not insist that everyone walk through the same territory. Umbanda, as we will see, comes in a wide range of flavors. Seu Silva's Umbanda is earthy, exuberant, pulsating with drumming and swirling with dancing. Dona Luciana's sessions are much quieter, allow-ing her exquisitely theatrical spirits to occupy center stage, almost like a series of one-woman plays. Some centers are very New Age. Others feature lengthy readings from Allan Kardec's spiritualist writings and the New Testament. One I became acquainted with was organized like a charity clinic: visitors "checked in" at the front desk, a nurse-like figure took case histories, and appointments were made. I was introduced to, but never worked with, an Umbanda center that shared space and occasionally ritual with followers of the Santo Daime religion, which employs an hallucino-genic tea (ayahuasca, also known as jurema, originally from Indians of the Amazon region and Northeastern Brazil) in their rituals; in fact, most of those Umbandistas at that center were also in Santo Daime. Though there have been a number of "federations" of Umbanda over the years, and it was even once a legal requirement to obtain a license from a federation to operate, there is no central authority, no Pope or synod or convention, to impose uniformity. There is an Umbanda path for almost any traveler.

Third, Umbanda offers a rich array of symbols and metaphors—like the path—and theoretical frameworks (reincarnation, karma, spiritual protectors and tormentors, orixás that hold one to a bargain or else, for example) with which to make sense of life or, perhaps more precisely, to make of one's life a compelling, coherent narrative. That, and to invest the material world of daily life with meaning and spirit—to undo what Max Weber called modernity's "disenchantment of the world." Umbanda reenchants the world, and that, to answer my professor's question, is a large part of what draws millions of people from all walks of life to Umbanda. It is that that is the subject of much of the rest of this book.

CHAPTER 3

Mistura (Mixture)

When you plant a cutting from a root in the ground, the plant that shoots forth is a clone, a true copy of one parent, unmixed. It is new life, but it is equally old life made new, unchanged in its essence and in its every detail. At the House of Father John they say that a warrior and sorcerer from Angola, Father John, planted a root from Africa in the ground where his house now stands. He hid that root on his body when he was captured by slave traders in Africa and sold into slavery in Brazil. In one version of the myth, he years later planted the root in his last free act before slave hunters recaptured him following an escape. From that root, they say, grew the Umbanda that they practice there.

People at the House of Father John express pride and admiration for the purity of the traditions reborn metaphorically from Father John's root. Unlike many Umbanda centers, Father John's is unmistakably African in its aesthetics and ritual practices. At Father John's, initiates undergo long periods of ritual seclusion, the African orixás are prominently featured, the floor is packed dirt, blood sacrifice is of paramount importance, and the dancing and the drumming are just what one hears and sees at the most traditional houses of Candomblé. As Zé puts it, "Here at the House of Father John, we have pure Angola, *Omolocô*.[1] Most other places mix everything up, but here there is foundation, a root." Africa, specifically Angola, in the heart of Rio de Janeiro.

But one sees things and hears things at the House of Father John that the young warrior and sorcerer could have never seen or heard in Angola. There are images of the Catholic saints everywhere. People come seeking advice and intervention from the spirits of old slaves and Brazilian Indians. The spirits often couch their counsel in terms of karma, reincarnation, and the nineteenth-century Spiritist doctrines of Allan Kardec. One medium receives a gypsy woman spirit who reads palms and tarot cards; another medium, when not in trance, relates the orixás to the archetypes of Karl Jung. Zé himself points out that the Angolan names of the *Inkeces* (deities) have been replaced by the Nagô (Yoruban, from slaves imported from what is now Nigeria) names for the orixás. And yet, for Zé, the Umbanda at the House of Father John grows true to its Angolan roots.

Brazil is a land of *mistura*, of mixture. From the quintessential dishes of Brazilian cuisine—for example, the stews of fish, tomatoes, hot peppers, and palm oil—to the eclectic genius of Brazilian literature and plastic arts and music, to the problematical myth of racial democracy by way of miscegenation, there is mixing, recombination, taking from here and there to make something that could be nowhere else. Brazilian culture, it seems, is a bricolage, to borrow Claude Lévi-Strauss's famous metaphor.[2] A *bricoleur* takes whatever is at hand—odds and ends, a length of pipe, the old bicycle gear, the two by four—whatever bits of the past can be imaginatively combined to meet the practical needs of the present. That is nowhere more true than with Umbanda, in which everything from Angola to Spiritism to Jung and the New Testament simmer away in a hundred different recipes.

Umbanda is a bricolage, but it is not a haphazard one. The parts left in and left out, the ways disparate elements of Spiritism and African religions, Catholicism, New Age, and myriad other sources combine, dynamically reflect history, ideology, and politics at all levels, from the personal to the national. Umbanda is a mistura, but, more than that, it is misturas, plural, some strikingly different than others, and these differences are rooted deeply in the contradictions—social, historical, and cultural—from which Umbanda springs. This chapter looks at how Umbandistas blend their Umbanda in different ways, and why, and about what those different misturas look and feel and taste like, and what they might mean.

HISTORICAL ROOTS

The story of Father John and the planting of his root may be mythical, but it is rooted in historical reality. The African roots of Umbanda are undeniable, and the story of Umbanda, along with those of other Afro-Brazilian religions, must begin with at least a brief discussion of certain aspects of Brazilian slavery. Some are dramatized in Father John's story, others passed over, and yet others expressed only metaphorically, but all are crucial to the formation of all Afro-Brazilian religions, including Umbanda.

From the very first Portuguese incursions in Brazil in the sixteenth century, until the so-called Golden Law finally brought abolition in 1888, slavery was the core fact of Brazilian life. Slaves, freed slaves, and their descendents provided the bulk of labor in the sugar, mining, and coffee industries, as well as in urban areas, where they worked as artisans, craftsmen, stevedores, domestic servants, carpenters and masons, messengers, and unskilled laborers. For most of the period, Africans and their descendents, whether black or of mixed ancestry, constituted the majority of the population. And for most of that period, the majority of blacks were slaves.[3]

The sheer magnitude and duration of the slave trade contributed greatly to the perpetuation of African religious traditions in Brazil. Precise numbers can never be known, but it is now generally agreed that around three and a half to four million Africans were brought to Brazil.[4] The trade did not end until after 1851 and, in fact, during the final five years of the trade nearly a quarter of a million Africans were imported (60,000 in 1848 alone).[5] Traditions that might otherwise have died out through acculturation—as largely occurred with African religion in North America—were continually recharged by thousands and tens of thousands of new arrivals every year, bearing within them and between them their natal cultures, constituting a living bridge of symbols, practices, minds, and bodies connecting Brazil with Africa.

By and large those brought to Brazil were people of medium- to large-scale societies, of kingdoms and chiefdoms, and the religions reflected this. It is true that much of their traditional practice centered on lineages and local communities, but even at that level belief and ritual were imbedded in larger systems. There were religious specialists; a division of ritual labor including drummers, dancers, novices, initiates, priests, and diviners; interdependent groups, each devoted to particular orixás; and those learned in the complex mythologies. This was truest of the West African religions, such as the Nagô (Yoruba) tradition that would later lend the names of its deities to Umbanda, but in all events even a considerably pruned down tradition required a critical mass of people and some time and space. Large-scale production on sugar and coffee plantations brought together significant numbers of slaves and, at least occasionally, afforded them the necessary conditions, and time, for ritual practice. (By law, slaves were given Sundays off and one more day a week to tend their own crops. How rigorously this was observed is open to question.) Perhaps more significant was the fact that so much of Brazilian slavery was urban; cities like Rio de Janeiro and Salvador, where for a very long time the majority of the population consisted of slaves and freed slaves, and where a complexly articulated system of occupations, combined with labyrinthine urban spaces[6] and the officially sanctioned institutions of Catholic brotherhoods for blacks, constituted fertile soil for the transplanted roots of African religion.[7]

The massive and enduring slave trade and the demographics of urban centers and large plantations may have contributed to the survival of African religion, but they also contributed to mistura. The cultural and religious diversity of the slave population was substantial. While a majority of slaves in Rio de Janeiro, like Father John, either came from or were descended from those who came from the Bantu regions of present day Angola and Congo, very large numbers of Brazilian slaves came from West Africa, and there were significant but much smaller contingents from Mozambique. And within a broad category such as "Congo/Angola" or

"West Africa," numerous nations were represented.[8] Father John's root is a metaphor of fidelity to a specific religious tradition from a particular place and time, but those with whom he would have lived and suffered on that coffee plantation (which itself we can understand as a metaphor representing the demographic diversity of the slave population) could well have come from a number of different places. They would have had in common some widely distributed cultural traits, the terrible circumstances of their lives, the emergent culture of slavery, and a pidgin Portuguese to communicate with each other and with the whites. To the extent that they shared a religion there in the slave quarters, it would have had to have been something intelligible and compelling for all, something that emerged in the give and take of people thrown together in the crucible of plantation life, a mistura. A root, yes, but to some degree a hybrid, a crossing, or a graft.

The dynamics of mistura in the cities no doubt differed in some important ways. The sheer numbers of urban slaves, and the relative mobility and potential for association enjoyed by at least some of them, afforded opportunities to practice religion with people from one's own tradition, especially under the cover of the Catholic religious brotherhoods, organized as they often were along ethnic lines.[9] In Salvador this led to the founding of several Candomblé centers, dating from the nineteenth century and flourishing today, remarkably faithful to specific traditions, such as Nagô and Gege from West Africa. While similar terreiros are not recorded for Rio until the early twentieth century, there can be little doubt that Afro-Brazilian religions were a vital presence before then. As in Salvador, the very large population of enslaved and free Africans met a necessary condition for keeping religious traditions alive. At the same time, the mobility and density of association assured that, as on the plantations, people of widely different geographical origins and cultural traditions would come together and potentially share and blend beliefs and practices—mistura.

And, of course, the cities were not just the province of slaves and their Afro-Brazilian descendents. Especially in Rio, and ever more so as the nineteenth century came to an end and the early twentieth century went on, the city was a place where not only Afro-Brazilian roots, but also folk Catholicism, Spiritism, and various esoterica circulated in a demographic stew of immigrants (from Portugal, Spain, Lebanon, and elsewhere), ex-slaves, and free born Afro-Brazilians (both urban and recently arrived from rural areas) mixing together, mostly poor, marginalized, and/or struggling for mobility—mistura. That is the ambience in which Umbanda took form—or rather its various forms, precisely in Rio de Janeiro.

This mixing of peoples and beliefs and practices was not haphazard. The bricoleur does not just throw random odds and ends together with no purpose in mind. His or her bricolage is an invention, born of necessity, an attempt at solving a problem. As the Brazilian anthropologist Renato Ortiz convincingly demonstrates in his study of the history of Umbanda, one of the central problems that practitioners of Afro-Brazilian religions faced—and by extension the inventors of Umbanda—was stigmatization, not only because of their departure from Catholic practice but, more importantly, the stigmatization that comes from association with blackness and poverty within a racist and classist society. This is key to understanding Umbanda and the various forms these misturas take. We might begin the unlocking by looking at another Umbanda origin myth, one very different than the story told of Father John and his root.

HAIL ATLANTIS

My conversations with Seu Gomes's spirits were the high points of my evenings at the House of Saint Benedict. They were certainly more congenial than the conversations I had with Dona Linda, the leader of the group; Elena (Dona Linda's daughter and also a medium); Cici; and Seu Gomes in the sitting room before sessions. Cici, a thoughtful, perceptive, pleasant, and expressive conversationalist who taught me so much during our drives out to the House of Saint Benedict, would be quiet and withdrawn as Seu Gomes would go on and on in minute detail about the most esoteric doctrines, convoluted discourses that none of us could quite follow. Those performances always left my brain scrambled, though I did actually learn a lot about so-called esoteric Umbanda. But they were much better than the political discussions, in which Dona Lisa and Elena, nostalgic for the dictatorship (this was 1991, six years after the end of military rule), sorely tested my diplomatic skills and self-restraint with barrages of the most reactionary opinions imaginable. To their credit, they listened patiently and never became upset at my objections to reinstituting a police state or worse. They considered me benighted, good hearted, but hopelessly naïve. To paraphrase Dona Linda, my liberal ideas were all fine and good for the advanced countries of North America and Europe. But "unfortunately here in Brazil the masses are at a primitive level, swayed by the communists, and they must be controlled with an iron hand." Even more disturbing than their rhetoric was the reminder that very nice people—and these are very nice people—can hold the most virulently dangerous prejudices.

Be that as it may, Seu Gomes's spirits were a delight. They were playful, twinkly-eyed, erudite, funny, and, more often than not, our conversations would take totally unexpected and charming turns. There was for instance his exu spirit, Marabô. Exus like Marabô generally fit the Catholic category of souls in purgatory, though quite often their sins are mortal. Seu Gomes's Marabô, an elegant and witty fellow with a wealth of knowledge regarding French history, which he was more than willing to share, was a nineteenth-century Parisian doctor who out of pity for young well-born ladies whose reputations and futures would be otherwise ruined, performed a number of abortions. He would tell historical anecdotes of Robespierre, Cardinal Richelieu, and Napoleon, along with his own recollections of Bohemian nights full of absinthe and worldly women. Seu Gomes's old slave spirit, Mané,[10] took a special interest in supporting my research with information. Mané was a very interesting character, to say the least. Although he identified himself as an old slave, he was unlike any other old slave spirit I knew. Most of the old slaves speak in ways that recall the pidgin that a Father John might have spoken, often with missing sounds, changes of one sound for another, misarticulations suggestive of missing teeth; they can be difficult to understand. They speak wisely, in their stereotypically creaky, wheezy old voices; their horizons encompassed the slave quarters, the plantation, or the mine, and memories of Africa. That was not Mané. Mané's diction was perfect, his voice deep and liquid, and he talked about esoterica of all kinds—Rosicrucians, the Cabal, New Age—jazz, popular science, and, like Gomes's Marabô, he had more than a passing interest in French history and culture. (I have since wondered about his name—should I spell it Mané or Manet?)

One night we were talking about the origins of Umbanda. He agreed with me that Umbanda came to Brazil from Africa by way of the slaves, but not quite in the way I thought. There was more to the story. Here is Mané's version (a composite, based on a full version he told one night, with details from other, partial tellings) of the origin of Umbanda:

Long ago on a far away planet they called Cabal lived a race of beings as advanced in comparison to us as we are to monkeys. It seems that long, long ago the highest wise men of the planet Cabal took up the charitable mission of spreading truth and enlightenment outward to all the other inhabited planets in the universe. They selected their brightest, most educated and spiritual young people and sent them forth in all directions on spaceships capable of light speed travel, so that they could search indefinitely for peopled planets; as Einstein demonstrated, time and therefore aging stops when one reaches those velocities.[11] One such ship happened upon Earth, a raw and savage place inhabited by brutes lacking all but the rudiments of culture and language. The Cabalan missionaries set to work, the fruits of which we see in the invention of writing and mathematics, the Neolithic revolution, and the almost simultaneous invention of civilization in Syria, Egypt, and China and, a little later, in the New World. The center of it all, their home base, as it were, was Atlantis, from which all spiritual, technological, and intellectual progress radiated. Unfortunately, a foolish experiment with nuclear power by arrogant scientists ended catastrophically, destroying Atlantis and its Cabalic civilization. A few citizens managed to survive, clinging to flotsam and drifting to black Africa, the one corner of the world the Cabalic enlightenment had not even touched. They [the survivors] weren't the best minds of Atlantis, but they were far above the Africans. They introduced metallurgy, counting, and law—albeit, in simplified form, in deference to the limited capacities of the African people. They also introduced their Spiritist religion, which they called Umbanda after the fundamental vibration Om. Unfortunately, the Atlantans soon succumbed to disease, violence at the hands of the natives, and the sheer despair of being surrounded by such barbarism. As a result, the Africans never advanced very far, and, even worse, the sublime Umbanda became mixed with fetishism, superstition, and generally barbaric practices. And that was what was brought to Brazil with the slaves. There was much truth and enlightenment in their religion—the parts from Cabal, by way of Atlantis—but much error and primitivism, from Africa. Our mission is to purge Umbanda of those impurities. So Umbanda, the real Umbanda, isn't an African religion; true Umbanda is Umbanda without Africa.

Mané tells the story with twinkling enthusiasm, delighting in its twists, the evocations of Atlantis and space travel and Einstein, the mapping of ancient history (and para-history) onto his grand tale of Umbanda. When he would tell it, and when I recount it for my students or my readers, I always feel a certain vertigo at the gaping chasm between his playful telling and the stark racism permeating the tale.

Mané's story is unusual in claiming an extraterrestrial origin for Umbanda, but it is by no means unique in minimizing, denying, or denigrating the role of black Africans. Other stories trace Umbanda to ancient Egypt, the Aztecs, or the Incas. It seems that the African root that Father

John planted in his last moments is one that Mané, and his medium, would just as soon tear out of the ground. Its fruit, it seems, threatens to spoil their mistura.

DEPRAVED IMAGINATIONS, GROSS INSTRUMENTS, AND TORPID LEWDNESS

Umbanda, as a mixture of Spiritism and Afro-Brazilian traditions actually called Umbanda by its practitioners, seems to have originated around the turn of the century in Rio de Janeiro. Rio then as now was a sprawling, complex, convoluted place, and in its nooks and crannies innumerable persons pursued spiritual power, healing, and meaning in diverse ways—again, true today. Paulo Barreto, a journalist of the time who went by the name of João do Rio and was drawn to the vibrant life of the margins, the night, the suburbs, and the slums that lay off the beaten track of official reporting, tells of Afro-Brazilian religion (including Islam), Comtean Positivists, evangelical Protestants, Maronites, Satanists, and Spiritists; in short, he gives us a glimpse into a flourishing marketplace of religious persuasions.[12]

Barreto's accounts of Afro-Brazilian practices have a peculiarly clandestine flavor, as if visiting a terreiro or a center were a vice, like slipping across the tracks for a night of jazz, drinking, and shadowy encounters. In fact, it was a kind of vice for respectable persons, like the educated journalist he was, or like the society ladies sneaking in via the back door for magic spells and the thrill of being among the exotic, black other. Afro-Brazilian religion was at that time heavily stigmatized. The Catholic Church forbade it, the press ridiculed it, and the police repressed it with greater or lesser degrees of brutality, including violent orgies of desecration and head banging of the sort fictionally depicted by the great Brazilian novelist Jorge Amado,[13] who lived through some especially repressive decades in Salvador. The police in Rio even displayed drums, images, costumes, and other ritual items seized during its raids on the terreiros, trophies from the "war against fetishism and black magic," as they called it.[14]

No doubt this repression was part of a larger imperative to control, intimidate, contain, and humiliate the Afro-Brazilian masses, but it seems that Afro-Brazilian religion in particular epitomized everything frightening, backward, degraded, and dangerous in the African heritage of the nation, a threat and an insult to moral order, good customs, and modern thinking. Writing two decades before abolition, the antislavery writer Joaquim Manoel de Macedo shared the visceral revulsion of the elite toward Afro-Brazilian religion:

The pagoda is usually a solitary house; the priest is an African slave, or some worthy descendent and disciple of same . . . The ceremonies and the mysteries are of the most incalculable variety, depending on how unbridled the imagination of the liars . . .

The gross instruments reminiscent of the savage festivals of the Brazilian Indian or the Negro from Africa sound; one sees rustic talismans and ridiculous symbols. The priest and the priestess ornament themselves with feathers and emblems and living colors. [They] prepare . . . unknown infusions of nauseating roots, almost always or sometimes rotten; the priest breaks into a frenetic, terrible, convulsive dance . . . The priestess goes around like a lunatic . . . [after an hour of] contortions, demonic dances, anxiety, and crazed activity . . . [she] announces the arrival of the genie, the spirit, the god of sorcery, for which there are twenty names, each one more brutal and burlesque.

. . . The obscene negress and her partner move lewdly. Interrupting their violent dance, they carry to each and all the vase or gourd containing the beverage, telling them to "drink pemba" and each one takes a swig of the dangerous and filthy pemba. Those who are sick from sorcery, the candidates to the office of sorcerer, those who use sorcery for good or bad ends subject themselves to the most absurd, repulsive and indecent ordeals, and to the most squalid of practices.

The bacchanal is complete; with the cure of the bewitched, with the torments of the initiations, with the concession of remedies and the secrets of sorcery are mixed the firewater and, in the delirium of all, in the infernal flames of depraved imaginations, are evidenced, almost always shamelessly, an unchecked, ferocious, and torpid lewdness.

All this is hideous and horrible, but that is how it is.[15]

Stripped of its lurid, breathless, language—lunatic! demonic dances! obscene negress! brutal and burlesque! torpid lewdness!—elements of Macedo's description fit with scenes I have observed in Afro-Brazilian Umbanda, such as that practiced at the House of Father John: there are infusions and dancing culminating in ecstatic possession, and costumes, and dramatic entries of mediums possessed by the orixás. Absent are the depravity, squalor, chaos and ignorance that Macedo sees, suggesting that those qualities are not in the scene, but inscribed on the glasses through which he observes. But that is beside the point; what Macedo's account really crystallizes is the depth and shape of the stigma heaped on Afro-Brazilian religion. Dealing with this stigmatization plays an important role in how different Umbanda centers constitute their mistura. Tales of Umbandas that come from outer space or ancient Egypt are obvious stories of denial, but even in Afro-Brazilian Umbanda, where stories of culture heroes like Father John valorize African roots, the kinds of prejudices expressed in the words of a Macedo or a João do Rio or by the nightsticks of the police decades and decades ago leave their traces: for example, in a certain prudishness about dress and comportment (a sign at Father John's: No shorts, no miniskirts, no low-cut or midriff-revealing tops, no smoking; and though there is no sign, it is made clear when it happens: no flirting); a watchful eye on the playful and sometimes lustful exu and pomba-gira spirits, so that their antics don't get out of hand; an insistence that only good is served at the House of Father John's—an insistence on goodness and propriety general to Umbanda but one that the spirits themselves sometimes problematize and relativize as they deal with the messy world of everyday reality.[16]

Beyond the stories of Atlantis and the mediums with long pants under their white dresses so that nothing too much might show when they twirl and dance possessed by the goddess of the wind, the prejudices about savagery and ignorance—code words for African, of course—probably contributes to one of the outstanding features of Umbanda, of whatever shade: the incorporation of Spiritist practices and discourses.

A STRANGER IN THE NEST AND THE MENTORS
OF THE SUPERIOR ASTRAL PLANE

The exu Marabô's revelation (see Chapter 1) of the true cause of my stuttering as the lingering effects of the guillotine on a freethinker, is one of many instances in which Umbandistas invoke past lives, karma, and reincarnation to make sense of selves and circumstances. Cici tells a story about her relationship with one of her sons: it seems that this son, from very early on, was somehow different than the rest of the family. Aloof, a bit of a loner, contrary, he presented a striking contrast to the warm, easygoing, cooperative temperament of his siblings and parents. He was, as Cici put it, "a stranger in the nest," like a jaybird hatched from an egg slipped surreptitiously into a robin's nest. A manageable problem during childhood, things spiraled during adolescence and Cici, especially, found herself in repeated crises with her son. The usual remedies—psychologists, family counseling, and so forth—were ineffective, and so Cici, finally, sought out an Umbanda center. It seems that the metaphor about the "stranger in the nest" was quite right, according to the spirit she consulted. We tend to meet up with the same especially significant persons, he explained, in different guises and circumstances, over numerous reincarnations, because we flow in the same spiritual currents. "Your family has been a family together several times, and each member has honed his or her place, has learned to live harmoniously together, as a result. Except for that son. He is indeed a stranger. Some spiritual eddy tossed him in with you; maybe the higher powers are testing you, to see how charitable you are, if you will welcome him and love him despite the difficulties. And maybe they are doing this to show you how wonderful your family is. Certainly this is an optimal opportunity to build positive karma."[17] According to Cici, this new perspective improved matters "a hundred percent"—there were still difficulties, but knowing where they came from, a rationale from which to act, made all the difference, and she now sees her son not as a stranger but as a gift.

The spirit's advice—full of references to reincarnation, karma, spiritual currents and eddies, the inscription of past life stories onto present living—comes to Umbanda by way of Spiritism. Cici was not new to Spiritism, though she was new to Umbanda, when she sought out the spirit's help. Growing up, her family, nuclear and extended, included many Spiritists. But Spiritism wasn't her cup of tea—too abstract, too intellectualized. In Umbanda she found a more down-to-earth, emotionally satisfying spirituality. Ronaldo, Dona Luciana's nephew, also had a background in Spiritism; in his case he spent years attending a Spiritist *mesa* in downtown Rio. Fascinated with the esoteric doctrines, impressed with its wisdom and "purity," Ronaldo maintains an enormous respect for Spiritism—in fact he bluntly asserts that it is more "elevated" and "evolved" than Umbanda—but finds that Umbanda, while not as intellectually rigorous, is for him much more satisfying.

Brazilian Spiritism, so influential in Umbanda and a significant contemporary presence in its own right, has as its source the writings of Hippolyte Léon Denizard Rivail (1803–1869). A Frenchman who studied science, medicine, pedagogy, and grammar, Rivail is reputed (by his followers) to have been a hard-headed materialist, empirical and skeptical in his thinking. Around midcentury, Rivail developed an interest in hypnotism and psychic phenomena, especially the supposed communication carried out with spirits at séances. Rivail explored the spiritual universe through a kind of questionnaire methodology, posing questions to the dead during séances. The result was a detailed description of the nature of spirits, the Beyond, the dynamics of reincarnation, and the relationship between spirits and living people. Rivail published his findings under the name of Allan Kardec. Kardec's books, along with the New Testament, are the core scriptures of Brazilian Spiritism. In Brazil, the Spiritist movement that followed is often called Kardecismo.

Spiritist sessions are called mesas, or "tables." Participants are seated around a table. Sessions begin with a prayer and a lecture, elaborating on Spiritist metaphysics and ethics. Spirits are then invited to descend. As in Umbanda, these speak through the mediums, offering advice and instruction. They are not, however, typically the spirits of old slaves and Indians; they tend to be educated, often illustrious: doctors, philosophers, artists, even famous historical figures such as Victor Hugo and Benjamin Franklin. These illuminated spirits share their wisdom from Beyond with the mesa. Occasionally, disturbed spirits make uninvited appearances; these are counseled, consoled, and sent on their way. Helping such lost souls, along with giving to the poor, is considered charity, the ethical mission of Spiritism, and it goes hand in hand with the quest for enlightenment.

Despite the fact that the Spiritist invocation of spirits is deeply offensive to official Catholic morality—and, in fact, the church consistently condemned Kardecismo—Spiritism never faced the intense stigmatization and repression experienced by followers of Afro-Brazilian religion. As David J. Hess points out in his study of Spiritism in Brazil, Kardec's Spiritism rejected such Catholic teachings as the divinity of Christ and the Trinity, while its mediumistic practices and its doctrine of reincarnation were anathema to the church, but its ethical and moral orientation were explicitly Christian.[18] Embodying ideals of progress and evolution, set down in erudite prose, and, last but not least, hailing from France, unrivalled font of culture and learning in the late nineteenth-century Brazilian imagination, Kardec's teachings found an immediate and enthusiastic following among elite sectors of Brazilian society. João do Rio, writing around the turn of the century, maintains that the first Spiritist center in Brazil opened in 1865, no later than its French counterpart, and he cites a Spiritist friend to the effect that if Paris has a hundred thousand Spiritists, Rio has nearly as many.[19]At the very time that Afro-Brazilian religions were stigmatized and repressed, Spiritism enjoyed high prestige. João do Rio mentions generals, admirals, and doctors who openly identify themselves as Spiritists, those being but a small portion of the thousands of, as he puts it, "our most lucid minds" involved with Kardecismo.

It is not surprising but certainly interesting that at least some people involved in Afro-Brazilian religions would explore the possibilities of a synthesis with Spiritism. The practice of mistura was already established; why not add Spiritism—and its prestige—to the assorted bricolages of orixá worship, folk Catholicism, backwoods curing and divining, and esoterica from various sources? As for why, there were no doubt a number of positive reasons, but one stands out for its ideological and pragmatic significance. That is, the incorporation, or appropriation, of Spiritism promised a radical repositioning of Afro-Brazilian religion within the stratified and contested social geographies of class and race. Another Umbanda origin myth, this one grounded in relatively recent events, suggests some dimensions of this struggle. Below is my translation of an account given by an Umbanda writer, Israel Cysneiros, who goes by the cult name Omolubá:

> The mentors of the superior astral plane . . . organized a movement to combat the negative magic that was spreading with frightening speed.
>
> There were formed then, at this time, the phalanxes of spiritual workers in the form of caboclos [spirits of Brazilian Indians] and pretos velhos [old slaves, Afro-Brazilian spirits] in order that [the message] be more easily interpreted by the masses. In the Spiritist sessions, however, these caboclos and pretos velhos were not accepted . . .

On the 15th of November, 1908, there appeared at a session of the Spiritist Federation in Niteroi, then under the direction of José de Gomes, a young man of 17 years . . . by the name of Zélio Fernandes de Morais . . .

Zélio was invited to participate at the table. When the proceedings began, spirits who identified themselves as slaves and Indians manifested themselves. The director warned them to leave. At that very moment, Zélio felt himself overcome by a strange force and heard his own voice demanding to know why the messages of blacks and Indians were not accepted, and if they were considered backward simply because of their color or their social class . . . one of the mediums asked the spirit to identify himself, in consideration of the fact that he appeared enveloped in an aura of light . . .

"If you wish to know my name, . . . then try this one: I am the caboclo Seven Crossroads, because for me all roads are open!"

He announced his mission: to establish the basis of a religion in which the spirits of Indians and slaves would come to fulfill the will of the Astral. The next day . . . [he would] found a temple, symbolizing the true and total equality that must exist between men.[20]

This myth is widely known among Umbandistas. I heard numerous versions at various Umbanda centers. The reported events have some basis in recorded fact. Zélio de Morais was a real person. Diana Brown, an anthropologist who did extensive survey research on Umbanda in the late 1960s, actually interviewed him.[21] In the early decades of the twentieth century (Diana Brown places it around 1920; Cysneiros' account gives 1908 as the crucial moment), Zélio founded the Spiritual Center of Our Lady of Piety at a place known as the Waterfall of the Macacu Tree, across the bay from Rio in Niteroi.[22] He would later move his temple to the center of Rio, where it continued to flourish even after his retirement in the 1960s.

Its factual basis notwithstanding, the story is mythical in at least four important ways. First, it presents as one unique, bounded, discrete episode the synthesis or mixing of Spiritism with Afro-Brazilian religion. Surely this happened in many places, among many individuals, over a span of time. I cannot prove this by citing eyewitness accounts, but given the spirit of mistura, the restless exploration, incorporation, recombination, and reinterpretation of symbols from widely diverse sources that pervades Umbanda now as it pervaded the Rio scene at the turn of the century, to think otherwise seems unreasonable. Contrary to the myths, Umbanda, like fire, was not invented just once.

Second, hidden in this myth is a claim to legitimacy—not for all Umbanda, but for a certain kind of Umbanda, one cleansed of "superstition" and "negative magic." Variously referred to as "Pure Umbanda" or "White Umbanda" this is an Umbanda more or less de-Africanized, the kind of Umbanda that the old slave Mané holds out as the goal of his medium's work. This is the Umbanda of the House of Saint Benedict. As Diana Brown points out, the founders of this strain of Umbanda disproportionately come from the "middle sectors"—military officers, bureaucrats, the professions, and below these—but still respectably above the bottom—teachers, skilled laborers, clerical and commercial workers, and those who would aspire to middle status by internalizing bourgeois values.[23]

Third, the story mythically alludes to deep ideological tensions and contradictions that continue to shape Umbanda today. On the one hand, the myth protests the racist exclusion of the old slaves and Indians from the Spiritist session—and on the other hand charters a new religion that would exclude the "superstition" and "negative magic," code words for Afro-Brazilian traditions. In glorifying Seven Crossroads and his spiritual colleagues of color, the myth valorizes the culture and being of the Brazilian masses—but sets forth a paternalistic project, whereby the "mentors of the Superior Astral Plane" would guide the benighted masses by using characters and language appropriate for the "humble classes."

The myth recognizes and protests the fact that the masses, symbolized by the old slaves and caboclos, are denied their places at the table, but the solution it proposes does not overturn the table, does not demand equal rights, not revolution, not even the reform of Spiritism. Zélio founds instead a table for the masses, and leaves the elite undisturbed in their temple of privilege.

Finally, this story is a myth (like Mané's story) in which legitimacy comes from above, from outside, from someplace radically removed from where one has come. Can that be any more different than the story of Father John's root?

PURITY, MIXTURE, AUTHORITY

Each of the origin myths I have cited makes a claim to authority based on purity. Father John's Umbanda sprouts forth from, literally, an African root. Mané has enlisted in the crusade for an Umbanda cleansed of everything "primitive" and "debased," the pure Umbanda disembarked from the planet Cabal. And Zélio de Morais brings the gift of Umbanda straight from the mentors of the Superior Astral Plane. And yet Umbanda, in all its variants, is mistura, always a blending of elements and influences, the most notable being Afro-Brazilian traditions and Spiritism, more or less permeated by Catholic symbols and ethics. A paradox: on the one hand, Umbanda's dynamism lies precisely in its restless incorporation and invention and reinvention, its exuberant mixedness; on the other, its very inventedness and mixedness seem to engender insecurities about authenticity and genuineness. The myths seek to ground these inventions in deep, deep tradition—or deep space.

The diversity of Umbanda mixtures also motivates anxiety. Voices in the flourishing Umbanda press regularly bemoan the lack of uniformity, the astonishing range of practices and understandings. One can see the point: surely the fruits of Father John's root and the gift of the Cabalan spacemen do not belong in the same basket? There have been over the years—for well over half a century, really—numerous attempts by various currents within Umbanda to establish the hegemony of their version of how things are to be done, of what things are supposed to mean. Congresses have been convened, federations launched—and counter-federations launched in their wake—certificates and licenses granted, all in an attempt to standardize, to homogenize, Umbanda. These efforts have met with no, or very limited, success. One reason is suggested by the origin myths discussed in this chapter: on the contested issues of race and class, diametrically opposed perspectives exist among those who practice Umbanda, and these differences cannot be simply erased. This fault line runs through every aspect of Umbanda—its tremors are felt in the sound and feel of ritual, the roles played by spirits and deities, in aesthetics and ethics, in the lives of practitioners.

Another reason these efforts have met with little or no success, equally important, involves the nature of authority and legitimacy within Umbanda. It is an overused and undertheorized concept, but leadership in Umbanda is largely based on individual charisma. The Umbanda leader is a virtuoso in the spiritual arts. Her power does not come from a federation, or a committee. It comes from the spirits that come to her, and with their guidance she mixes the Umbanda that holds sway in that place. As we shall see, most strikingly with Dona Luciana's spirits, there are profound and complex affinities between master mediums and their spirits; they are in a sense metaphors of one another. Each Umbanda center, each mixture, is as potentially unique as its guiding spirits and medium. And if one or more followers find the recipe unpalatable, they can leave and make their own mixtures (as Dona Luciana did), and if they attract followers—if they are imbued with charisma—another version of Umbanda is out there.

Chapter 4

The Old Slaves

People come to Umbanda to get help with their problems. Their problems may be physical—illness or injury—they may involve troubled relationships, problems with bosses or coworkers, money troubles, anxiety, anger, depression, or just bad luck, but, whatever the problem, the spirits are there to listen, advise, encourage, and intervene with their spiritual powers. The most beloved of these spiritual advisors are the pretos velhos, which literally means "old blacks" but which I gloss as old slaves. They are the spirits of Afro-Brazilian slaves. Most lived and died on plantations, though some toiled in the mines or in cities. Some were born in Brazil; others were brought to Brazil from Africa. Most of them are old; often attached to their given names are the kin terms "Father" or "Grandmother," by which they are affectionately addressed. Most of them carry the marks of age and injury, walking hunched over, stiff, with the help of canes; their voices tend to be creaky, and some shake with palsy. They are kind and patient and wise. They are talkers but even more they are listeners, puffing on their pipes and sometimes sipping sweet cheap red wine as they get to the bottom of things. This makes them great counselors; in fact, they are often called the "psychoanalysts of the poor." And they are martyrs, profoundly Christian in their sacrifice. They have suffered enormously at the hands of their fellow man, but their message is one of forgiveness, humility, and love. If slavery represents a metaphoric crucifixion, than the old slaves are metaphors of a kind of Christian ethos Nietzsche derided as "slave religion."

When I first began reading about Umbanda many, many years ago, before I ever actually met any old slaves, I found them troubling. They seemed to represent the worst kinds of stereotypes—creaking, dodder-ing, passive, cheek-turning Uncle Toms. Their forgiveness of the past sins of slavery symbolically represented acquiescence in the face of the contemporary status quo, in which most Afro-Brazilians are poor, most of the poor are Afro-Brazilian or of mixed ancestry, and life contin-ues as a purgatory and a crucifixion for many. Brazilian Uncle Toms, Brazilian Aunt Jemimas. What could be more retrograde? It read like a minstrel show.

But then I actually got to know, and in some cases know quite well, a number of old slaves. They weren't always what I expected, though my description in the opening paragraph is accurate for most. Beneath the ste-reotypes, I found dramas of good and evil, resistance and surrender, hope and despair, and critiques of how things were but, more importantly, how things are. The old slaves function in Umbanda as healers and counselors, but they are also the characters in dramatic narratives. These narratives can be, often are, critical, and can be, often are, nuanced explorations of power and powerlessness. Here are some of their stories.

CONGO KING

I never got to know much about the man who received the spirit known as Congo King during the afternoon sessions at Father John's. A tall, thin man, with dark skin and thin straight hair, he was polite but very, very reserved. Umbanda he would talk about, but my initial attempts at get-ting him to talk about himself seemed to make him uncomfortable. So I backed off. I made a point of greeting Mané (a nickname; his given name was Alberto) and asking his blessing and exchanging pleasantries when-ever I came to a session, figuring that over time he'd open up. Maybe he would have, maybe not. Some months after I met him, he started missing sessions, and soon stopped coming altogether. I asked about him a few times, but no one had much to say. "Seu Alberto? He's traveling—." "Seu Mané, he comes and goes—." I sensed there was something more going on, and I knew I would never find out what it was.[1]

My interest in Seu Mané was sparked by my connection to his old slave, Congo King. People bring their problems to the old slaves; I talked with Congo King about my work. He took it on himself to instruct me in what he knew. Wreathed in pipe smoke, sad, bloodshot eyes looking deeply into mine and then off into the distances of memory and cosmos, he would tell me about the orixás, about Umbanda, about the spirits. He described various herbal baths I could concoct to help with my research, to clear congestion, to calm my nerves. He told me about charity, that spiritual work must be done without thought of material reward, though, of course, if someone were to give the old slave a bottle of red wine or a plug of tobacco in gratitude, that would be kind. And on and on, a wealth of information. Congo King was often hard to understand. Like many old slaves, he spoke the dialect of a *boçal*, an Africa-born slave who learned a kind of pidgin Portuguese to get by. And then, every sentence or two, his tired, creaky voice would break, his breath and body wracked in a severe, convulsive stutter while his eyes sparked wide with fear. And then he would gather himself and go calmly on instructing me until the next attack.

Congo King never talked about his stuttering, and he was just as close-mouthed as Seu Mané about his personal history. I learned from him only that he had been a king in Africa, and then a slave somewhere in Brazil. He had no story to tell about himself, at least not in his actual words. His story instead was written on his body. Stiff joints, stooped back, the cane, the raspy breath—all spoke of a body ruined by too much work, too much punishment, too little food, and too many years. Most eloquent in his unspoken narrative, however, was the stuttering. It went beyond stammering and repetitions and blockages; it was elemental, seizure like, a sudden storm, a convulsive panic. I talked with others about it. What is it with Congo King's speech?

It was flipping on a switch. About this, people had lots to say. Congo King had been traumatized. Perhaps his brain had been damaged. People told of torture, of beatings, fingernails ripped out and eyes gouged out, brandings and scaldings, castrations and more. "Slavery did that to him, it's his cross, the marks of his crucifixion." "That is what they did to our ancestors"—that remark came from an older Afro-Brazilian woman; a young white woman told me: "That's what our ancestors did to them." And a young Afro-Brazilian man told me: "They say slavery is over, torture is over. That Brazil is a racial democracy. Don't believe it. Black men still catch it in the barracks of the military police!"

Congo King's stuttering struck a nerve.

THE SLAVE WOMAN ANASTÁCIA

While Congo King had little to say about his own personal history, he knew a story that crystallized the truth of the old slaves. This all came up one afternoon when I had sought Congo King's advice about a talk I was scheduled to give to some professors and graduate students in the anthropology program at the Federal University of Rio de Janeiro. I was really nervous, intimidated. I certainly didn't feel like much of an expert on Umbanda, the subject of my talk, and I was not very confident as a public speaker, especially in Portuguese. Congo King prescribed some ritual preparations to ensure success: "Abstain from sex and drinking the day and night before the talk. Take a regular shower in the morning, then wash thoroughly with the oily, black soap imported from Africa, known as *sabão de costa*. Then dress in freshly cleaned clothes. Light a candle to your guardian angel right before you leave home, asking seven times for protection and tranquility. During your talk, visualize these slave quarters where we are sitting now."

He then told me this story. If I wanted my listeners to understand about the old slaves, then I should tell them the story of the slave woman Anastácia. Claiming not to be much of a storyteller, Congo King outlined the plot, and urged me to get a copy of Anastácia's biography. That would be easy enough. Anastácia at this time (1991, three years after the centenary of Abolition) had become an important figure in Brazilian folklore. So much so that the Archdiocese of Rio removed her image from the

Museo do Negro (housed in the Church of the Lady of the Rosary and Saint Benedict in downtown Rio; Saint Benedict is the patron saint of black slaves) because it was becoming the focus of a "cult" and a popular movement toward the canonization of Anastácia. I went to a store not far from that church that sells beads, candles, esoteric books, professionally recorded Umbanda hymns, and images of saints, old slaves, and other spirits, and bought a book about Anastácia. There was a poster of Anastácia on the wall. She had very dark skin, close cropped hair, light blue eyes—and wore an iron muzzle. Besides the book, I would also view a miniseries about Anastácia at the home of friends who, like Congo King, enthusiastically endorsed the story.[2]

Somewhere in Africa, a blue-eyed girl is born. In some tellings she is a princess, in at least one a daughter of the orixás. One day she is visited by an orixá, who bestows on her the mission of bringing the power of their religion to the New World, where her people suffer in slavery. Soon enough, the young woman is captured and sold into slavery, ending up on a plantation in Brazil. Beautiful as she is, she becomes the object of her master's sexual obsession. He puts her to work in the manor house, close at hand and far from the backbreaking labor in the fields. She refuses his advances, however, and lust turns to vengeance; he sends her to the slave quarters, to live out her years working the fields. (In one version, the master takes out his frustrations by allowing his white visitors to rape Anastácia, resulting in numerous blue eyed offspring of various shades, certainly a biting metaphorical take on the myth of Brazilian racial democracy.) The master's wife, jealous of Anastácia, tells some lies, and the master, by now thoroughly corrupted by his own power and cruelty, decides to teach Anastácia a final lesson. He has her muzzled in iron. Time goes by. Anastácia uses the powers given her by the orixás to cure and comfort her people in the slave quarters. But eventually the cuts and gouges and abrasions from the muzzle lead to gangrene. As Anastácia agonizes, the master's young son takes sick. Dying, he is brought to Anastácia by his parents, who beg her forgiveness and her healing touch. Anastácia cures the boy, dying herself in the process. The master and his wife repent and seek redemption for their cruelty through a life of good works and charity.

While some readers may be put off by the sentimentality and melo-drama of the Anastácia story, it was for my informants a powerful and evocative myth. And Congo King was entirely correct: it is enormously helpful in understanding the old slaves. At one level this is a Christ story. Anastácia is perhaps the daughter of an orixá, a god; at the least she is chosen by the orixás to save her people. If Christ was born of a virgin, Anastácia, too, is a biological paradox, born with blue eyes. She is tempted, but does not give in. She heals the sick, and finally gives up her life—in agony—that others may live and be redeemed. Her end is the ultimate cheek turning and, indeed, the final emotional kick to this story comes when Anastácia triumphs over the master by taking the high ground of forgiveness as he begs on bended knee. The listener, identifying with Anastácia, triumphs vicariously. This must be especially powerful for the poor and downtrodden, and there are many of those in Umbanda, but satisfying also for almost anyone who has been wronged without redress. That may not be in the true Christian spirit, but one needn't be Nietzsche to read the ressentiment implicit in the story.

Another theme in this story is that of exile. Anastácia is born in a golden age, in an African paradise, a place of truth, justice, beauty, and plenty. The contrast to plantation Brazil could not be starker. It is as stark as the contrast between the way things ought to be, and the way things really are; again, this is a story about long ago, but it is also about today. There are other important themes—for example, the matter of sexual oppression, to which I will return in other old slave stories. But for now, I would point out one obvious symbol of oppression, the muzzle. Anastácia is silenced. In her silence she does good deeds, devoting her life to others. But the muzzle is her cross, and eventually her silence is her death. What does she say through her silence that speaks so movingly to Congo King, my friends who showed me the miniseries, and to millions of other Brazilians?

GRANDMOTHER CATHERINE

While race is a pervasive theme in old slave narratives, the tale of Anastácia hints at the role of sexuality—sexuality thoroughly entwined with race—in the construction of these characters. Anastácia is crucified—muzzled and raped—her sex is her curse, while her race compounds her powerlessness. Anastácia is black, but patriarchy and sexual violence transcends color; her story weaves together themes of slavery and themes of women, suggesting perhaps that they are one.

When I first met Grandmother Catherine, her medium Ronaldo (Dona Luciana's nephew) was still a young man. Grandmother Catherine, however, was very old. How old, I asked? With a coquettish giggle, she avoided the question. The fact that her medium was a "he" was rather unusual; perhaps out of a defensive sensitivity to stigmatization of Afro-Brazilian religions as attracting homosexual males, in many Umbanda centers men do not receive female spirits. But no one seemed uncomfortable with Ronald's performance. Indeed, his masterful use of falsetto and mannerisms made for a fascinating representation.

Grandmother Catherine was born in the slave quarters, on a plantation somewhere, some long time ago. Pretty and smart, she was plucked from the slave quarters at a young age to be the companion and confidant and eventual servant of the master's young daughter. Raised in the manor—the "big house," as they call it—she learned reading and music and the manners and morals of a young white lady, which of course she was not. But until she reached womanhood, it was "as if." And then, as with Anastácia, men lusted after her. But unlike Anastácia, she traded on that, living the high life, courtesan of the manor, a life of parties and finery and lovers. It all had to end. She aged, her beauty faded, and back she went to the slave quarters.

Grandmother Catherine lights up when she tells of her youth, about the parties and the lovers, but turns sad reflecting on the barrenness of it all, that she had no children, squandering herself in illicit pleasures, vanity, and egoism. The return to the slave quarters marked rock bottom. But it also marked a beginning, the end of her sexuality. She would now devote herself, not to herself, but to her fellow slaves. Catherine reports that she spent two years in the slave quarters giving "charity" (the same word Umbandistas use to describe the aid that spirits give, and the work that mediums do in channeling the spirits) for every year she spent in her life of debauch. She tended to the slaves' illnesses and injuries, taught them to read, taught them Christian morals, interceded on their behalf with the master. Not having any children of her own, she became a grandmother to all, and old slave to the slaves.

In her 1985 study of Umbanda, Paula Montero emphasizes the desexualization of the old slaves.[3] Neutered as it were by age and infirmity, the deeply cultural threat posed by black sexuality (in Brazil as in the United States, it would seem) is rendered harmless; the old slaves can take on the roles of nurturing, sympathetic, forgiving, embracing, loving grandparents. Sexless, and therefore toothless.

And yet not all the old slaves are sexless, and not all are toothless. First let me tell the story of one who is not sexless. Then I'll tell the story of one who is not toothless.

FATHER GERÔNIMO

I came to know Father Gerônimo at about the time I met Grandmother Catherine. While Ronaldo's Grandmother Catherine sat in one corner on her low stool, dispensing wisdom and healing, Father Gerônimo, "incorporated" in Dona Luciana, worked in the opposite corner. As characters they are quite different, but as artistic creations—I take the position that besides all the other things that spirits may or may not be, they are also aesthetic forms, cultural constructions shaped by the internal and external contexts and contingencies of the mediums who receive them— they have much in common as well. If the bare bones of Catherine's tale suggest a novel, a romance, and the fleshed-out performances of her medium remind one of scenes from a *telenovela* (soap opera) or a movie, that may be because they are steeped in popular representations of plantation life. Catherine seems almost to have stepped out of Bernardo Guimarães's nineteenth-century novel *A Escrava Isaura* (The Slave Isaura) and, in my imagination, I could place her in scenes from melodramatic period-piece telenovelas like *Sinha Moça*.⁴ Father Gerônimo, too, seems to have stepped out of a novel or onto a television screen during prime time.

Father Gerônimo's story also starts in the slave quarters, where he was born. Young Gerônimo strikes up a childhood friendship with the master's son. They grow up together, black and white but bosom buddies underneath it all, sharing adventure, good fortune, and bad. As with Catherine, though in radically different ways, the relationship with the master's child has sexual consequences. When Gerônimo reaches adulthood—a vigorous, virile adulthood—he is a big, strong man; his physical attributes and his favored status with the master result in his being chosen as a *reprodutor*, a human stud to sire the plantation's labor force (the historical plausibility of this is beside the point—the mythical resonance with themes of slavery, sexuality, friendship, and power is what counts). Father Gerônimo recounts this all with gusto, a certain braggadocio regarding his studliness, his potency, his carefree, work-free life of sex and adventure. (Perhaps it is important here to point out that his medium is an elderly woman; just as the role of Catherine allows her medium to imaginatively explore aspects of femininity, Father Gerônimo allows his medium entrée to a masculinized fantasy.) Father Gerônimo did regret that his children would sometimes be sold off, and that they would not live free. But life was good. He was as free as a slave could be.

There was one restriction placed on his behavior though. There was a beautiful slave, coincidentally named Catherine (not the same Catherine), with whom the master's son was infatuated. Of course, Catherine and Gerônimo (still a young man, young middle-aged at the oldest) fall in love. The affair is found out. Enraged, the master's son orders that his erstwhile best friend be tied to the trunk of a tree, where he proceeds to beat Gerônimo to death.

FATHER JOHN

Like Congo King, Father John was born in Africa (in Angola), captured
by slavers, and brought to Brazil where he suffered tremendously in captivity. He spent many, many years laboring on a plantation in the state of
Rio de Janeiro. He suffered torture but it did not break him. The Father
John I came to know speaks easily and directly; he is old but not decrepit,
humble but dignified.

There are lots of stories about Father John. They are not all consistent
as to the details of his life, but together they paint a clear picture of the
man. It is not a picture of the broken down, resigned victim (though he
is a victim and dies violently).

Like Congo King, Father John was a powerful man in Africa. Some
stories portray him as a heroic warrior who fought against the slave traders; one even tells that he was never enslaved at all, but died fighting for
his land and freedom. In other accounts, though, he is captured. Besides
being a warrior, Father John was a powerful sorcerer (if we can strip away
from that word the connotations of evil), with deep knowledge of the
ways of spirits and plants. As the slavers took him away, he managed
somehow to hide on his person the root of a plant embodying the knowledge and power of his religion. He kept it hidden through the passage and
through his years in captivity until, one day—in some versions he leads a
slave revolt, in others he just escapes alone—he and his root are free again,
fleeing and hiding out in the wooded mountains around Rio. Eventually,
of course, the slave hunters and their dogs track him down. As they close
in on him, he scratches a hole in the cold ground with his bare hands and
buries his root. In one version they tie him to the trunk of a great tree.
As the whip comes down, he gives a mighty thrust and the great tree and
Father John launch into the heavens. In other versions, less ballistic and
more poignant, they just beat him to death. But in either case, Father John
prevails in the ultimate sense, because he managed to plant his root, from
which his religion could sprout anew in Brazilian soil. And indeed, the
place where he planted his root, the stories go on, is just the spot where

two centuries or more later Seu Silva would build the Umbanda center at which Father John dispenses healing and wisdom and truth today.

THE ANCESTORS

To fully understand the old slave stories, to grasp why they are told with such delight and pathos, we must appreciate what the old slaves *are* for the people who come to Umbanda, at an emotional level. It is clear to me that the old slaves are dearly loved, spirits with whom people identify, from whom they take great comfort; they are shoulders to cry on, fonts of unconditional love. They are family.

The great French sociologist Roger Bastide, who devoted a life's work to Afro-Brazilian religions, points out that a vital part of those religions' traditions could not make the passage to Brazil.[5] These religions were not just about gods; they were about the thread of life that runs back through the living who are loved, who die, who become the ancestors who remain vital to spiritual life and to a sense of meaning in place. Ancestors are grounded in places, in villages and lands occupied by lineages in Angola and Congo and Yoruba land. Lineage is, in a fundamental sense, place, the place where generations are laid down one after the other through time. But with slavery, the ancestors stayed behind; they stayed home.

Gods are ideas, concepts; ancestors are as well, but they are concepts that are the fruit of flesh and blood. Slavery not only uprooted people from the places saturated by their ancestors, the demographics of slavery worked against the rebirth of the ancestral spirits in Brazil. Mortality was high; reproduction (the story of Father Gerônimo notwithstanding) low. Replacement of the labor force, if we can use that phrase in regard to slavery, was largely accomplished via importation. Biological reproduction, when it did occur, did not entail the cultural reproduction of lineage. Blood established no rights to lineage property, protection, or power; slaves had little or none of that, and lineages without those attributes are without substance. The celebration of ancestors, the cultivation of their spiritual role in daily life, as symbols of identity, as living presences in family and lineage life—that part of Father John's root, at least, could not sprout.

And yet the old slaves, representing those very people whose ancestry was wrenched away from them, also constitute a new form of ancestor cult, a reweaving of that essential thread of life that binds the departed to the present. The old slaves are not specific lineage ancestors; they are general, cultural ancestors. They symbolize the past not of clan X or clan Y, but rather the roots of Afro-Brazilians and the roots of Brazilians more generally (as one hears again and again, in various phrasings "all of us in Brazil are mixed, we all have at least a drop of African, a drop of Portuguese, a drop of Indian blood"). Symbolically, the old slaves represented generalized Afro-Brazilian ancestors.[6]

I was made most poignantly aware of this around three o'clock one Sunday morning. It was on the weekend that fell closest to May 13 that year, the day on which, in 1888, all slaves in Brazil were finally declared free. By that time there were more free than enslaved blacks, and the institution had been under siege for decades—importation was outlawed in 1830 and actually ended in the 1850s and there was a law passed in 1871 that declared free any baby born of a slave, and so forth. But there were still many, many slaves, and May 13, 1888, is a day of enormous significance. Umbanda celebrates this day with a ritual known as the feast of the old slaves; in most centers, the feast falls on the weekend nearest the actual day: work and commerce do not halt to commemorate abolition, as they do for World Cup games in which Brazil plays.

I was tired and glad for the refreshing cool of a winter night. Jorge and I stood near the drums watching as about thirty of the mediums, most in trance and all dressed as old slaves, sat on their little boxlike chairs around a big rectangle of white sheets on the ground. Leaves were strewn over the sheets, and there were big clay pots full of food—corn, okra stew with peppers and shrimp, boiled eggs, bananas, papayas, pineapples, oranges, even grapes (an expensive fruit in Rio), bean fritters, fish, yams, rice, and an enormous steel pot of black beans. The food had been brought down from outside in a joyous procession as the drummers played and everyone sang African words of which very few knew the literal meanings. The old slaves circled the food several times in a hobbling, shuffling dance, bent over on their canes, shaking with palsy. And then they sat to partake of the spiritual essence of the food. They seemed deep in memories; their eyes were far away. And then I noticed several of them were quietly weeping.

I turned to Jorge. Jorge, at the time in his vigorous early sixties, prized his roots. Samba and religion were big in his life. "Jorge," I said, "the old slaves are crying. Why are they crying?" He put a hand on my shoulder and leaned close. "They're crying because they're remembering. See, when they were in Africa, they never knew hunger. There was always plenty, and they were free. When our ancestors were brought over here—those ancestors we represent as old slaves like these—the worst thing about their lives was the hunger. Even worse than the beatings; you recover from those. But the hunger was always there. The food was terrible, just enough to keep them alive from one day to the next, sometimes not that. When they dreamed of freedom, of a good life, they dreamed of food. So they see this, this looks to them like heaven, like home. They cry because they remember how they suffered, and they cry because their descendents remember them and give them this. They cry from pain, they cry from happiness. They cry because they know we are free, which they couldn't be. That we have food, all we need."

Jorge's voice was cracking a bit and I stood silent with a lump in my throat. He went on. "See, things have really changed. We're free! We have plenty! Things have changed, right?" Jorge looked at me, and his eyes drew mine to look out at the better than one hundred people out there sitting on benches in the audience, waiting for the old slaves to finish taking in the spiritual essence of the food. Most were not regular visitors to the center. Most, I could tell from their clothing, were poor; many were too, too thin. Here they were, at three o'clock in the morning; they had sat on those benches for hours. To celebrate their ancestors, yes, but when their ancestors had their fill, they would get theirs, a feast of good, good food—protein and vitamins and fats and fibers—that comes very rarely for people in their circumstances. "Yes, my gringo friend," Jorge went on, his arm now on my other shoulder, holding me close, "things have changed but things have not changed so very much at all."

Thinking of the old slaves as ancestors opens three avenues to understanding their role as counselors and healers, the palette of emotions painting the relationships between these spirits and living people, as well as their ideological significance.

First, they literally represent the African slaves who are, in fact, the ancestors, in greater or lesser degree, of much of the Brazilian population. For Jorge, who considers himself thoroughly Afro-Brazilian, the connection is straight, undiluted—"these are our ancestors, our great-great-grandparents"; "when our people were brought from Africa"; "in Africa, where we came from"; his language makes this clear. Again, the phrase about all Brazilians having at least a drop of black, of yellow, of white blood suggests at least some degree of psychological connection to the old slaves as ancestors. Equally important, the old slaves represent the major historical drama in the formation of Brazil and Brazilians. They afford imaginative entry into the historical experiences of powerlessness, suffering, getting by, getting crushed, and finding redemption. The stories I have told here give only a snapshot of the range of different takes. There are Uncle Toms, but there are Nate Turners as well. No doubt the old slaves are stereotypes, but, at least in many cases, these stereotypes are developed and elaborated and nuanced as they are performed by mediums and, as their stories are talked about, they become the mutable, multifaceted figures of a living discourse.

Second, though the old slaves come from centuries ago, their fictive kin roles as grandmothers and grandfathers place them within a familiar and emotionally saturated cultural context. In Brazilian culture, the relationship to grandmothers, grandfathers, and elderly relatives is generally marked with affection, tenderness, and respect. The grandparent, the great aunt or great uncle, is likely to constitute a dependable source of sympathy, indulgence, wisdom, advice, and intercession on the child's behalf vis á vis power—that is, parents—from the child's earliest years. This is not always the actual case, and surely urbanization, mobility, and the myriad strains modernity places on familiar, affective ties has taken its toll, but it is deeply imbedded in the cultural psychology. The old slaves tap into this emotional resource and that emotional hunger.

Third, though ancestors are by definition removed in time, they are significant to the extent that they are a contemporary presence. This is most powerfully symbolized (and more than symbolized, *constituted*) through the language of flesh and blood. With the old slaves, of course, the flesh and blood is metaphorical; no one can trace their ancestry to Father Gerônimo. But even as a metaphor, the connection can be compelling, as can be seen in Jorge's comments. Beyond the real or imagined blood that ran through their—and runs through our—veins, ancestors feel what we feel, suffer what we suffer, they are as we are, and even though their actual historical circumstances may be much different, underneath, their lives makes sense to ours.

Jorge makes that poignantly clear in his lesson to me about why the old slaves cry. Their historic misery is akin to the contemporary misery of the very poor, its lineal ancestor in ways both real and metaphoric. What may not be so clear is that almost everyone who comes to Umbanda seeking the help of the old slaves is caught, or feels herself caught, in predicaments and contradictions for which the old slaves, these metaphorical ancestors, provide apt metaphors. The old slaves faced a hostile world—symbolized by the nearly all-powerful, capricious master—bereft of power. The hope and promise of youth, the noble, full and free being that one is and potentially can become—think of Congo King, or even Catherine—is robbed and crushed, bit by bit, by a system that already chose them as its victims. Open resistance, bold self-assertion—witness Father John—is noble, but suicidal. Gerônimo learns that in a regime of grossly unequal power, even friendship with the powerful is poisonous to the weak.

Looking at the situations many of those who come seeking the old slaves find themselves in, I am drawn again to Jorge's conclusions—things have changed but things have not changed so very much at all. Some are tormented by bosses they dare not stand up to, in jobs they can't leave, purgatories that are at least a shade cooler than the inferno of unemployment. Others, and some of the same ones, feel powerless, abused, and trapped in intimate relationships. Reality catches up and crushes the happy-go-lucky Gerônimos and Catherines. Dreams die, asphyxiated by lack of opportunity, by structures that work against dreamers in favor of those who already have it made. Not all the time, but at least often enough that it is how the world looks to many of those who come to Umbanda (and many who don't, of course). The old slaves have been there. The connection is empathic, and their advice is realistic, not revolutionary.

Caution, cunning, and compromise are critical to the survival strategies of the powerless. The bold assertiveness of the caboclo can get a slave killed—or a worker fired. I sat one evening listening as a young woman consulted with Catherine about the dirty politics in her office. She was fed up, especially with lies and abuse at the hands of a coworker, unfortunately a nephew of the boss. She had made up her mind—him or me. She was going to the boss the next day. Even a gringo like me could read the handwriting on that wall.

Catherine consoled, cajoled, held her hands, dried her tears, commiserated, but in the end turned her toward a strategy of conciliation and nonconfrontation. This coworker is insecure, he feels threatened by your competence. Put him at ease. Ignore his digs. Be sweet. Turn him into a friend. Understand the position your boss is in—that's his kin. Don't push him to take a stand. Make yourself even more valuable. Honey, not vinegar. And discreetly look for a new position.

We can interpret this advice—and much of the advice the old slaves give—as a call to capitulation. Which it is. And we can read a moral running through all of their stories: the weak lose, the powerful win, and we (you) are the weak. Submit. That too is a valid interpretation. But the advice and the stories carry a further message, one in tune with the old slaves as metaphorical ancestors.

Note that Catherine, Anastácia, and Congo King suffer their defeats and live out their lives in the slave quarters, the *senzala*, devoting their lives to serving their fellows. They are healers, counselors, wise persons, selfless contributors. They have turned away from confrontation with the system and turned their energies toward the reconstruction of a moral community, a place of justice, benevolence, nonviolence, good. Even Father John, unbowed, in his last act plants the root from which the old religion, and by extension the moral community, will spring forth. While the old slaves at one level are about accommodation—survival through humility—at another level they are about a human community where social relations are based on equality, mutuality, communication (they talk and talk!), empathy, the sacrifice of ego for the greater good. The senzala stands against the Big House, and it stands against the everyday savagery experienced by those on the bottom steps of the capitalist pyramid. It is founded on moral principles that are at once grounded in New Testament conceptions (turn the other cheek, practice charity, judge not, etc.), and rooted in a golden age, an Africa in which, as Jorge puts it, there was plenty for all. It is, indeed, the home of those ancestors exiled, like their Umbanda descendents, in a cruel new world.

CHAPTER 5

Cabocla Jurema

In describing the category of spirits known as caboclos, the anthropologist Diana Brown tells us that:

> Caboclos are collectively identified as unacculturated Indians, inhabitants of the Amazonian forests. They are men and women at the height of their powers and vitality, hunters and warriors who are arrogant, brave, and often somewhat vain. In describing the personality traits of caboclos, leaders and mediums at Umbanda centros repeatedly used the terms "proud," full of *força* (power), arrogant, aggressive, authoritarian, *mandão* (domineering). They are considered to be highly intelligent and talented specialists in curing and advising on a variety of problems.[1]

I had my first conversation with a caboclo toward the end of the second Umbanda session I attended in early June of 1986. The session took place in the apartment of Dona Luciana, to whom I had a week before been introduced by her niece who was acquainted with a colleague of mine. It was a small gathering. Dona Luciana and her nephew Ronaldo were there, along with a half a dozen or so visitors who had come, to borrow Diana Brown's phrase, seeking "curing and advising on a variety of problems." Besides myself, there was just one man among the visitors, perhaps in his midtwenties; the rest were women, ranging in age from their early thirties to late fifties/midsixties. I was the only foreigner. After a half hour or more of small talk in the living room, during which Dona

Luciana seemed to regard me with some skepticism, the session began. Dona Luciana and Ronaldo went into the bedroom and sang a number of hymns, referring to various orixás and caboclo spirits. Dona Luciana received in succession three different caboclos, who performed some necessary preliminary rituals, before she and Ronaldo finally received the two highly talented and intelligent specialists who would be advising and counseling that evening. One by one, the visitors were summoned to the bedroom to consult with the caboclos. I waited until last, because I needed no curing and my only problem was curiosity. Finally, after about an hour and a half, the last visitor, a tall, blonde woman in her forties, possessed of a wonderfully smooth, low voice, emerged from the bedroom and led me by the hand to introduce me to the cabocla Jurema.

I knew from reading any number of the little books written by followers of Umbanda that can be purchased in any bookstore,[2] or in the specialty shops that carry the candles, incense, images of saints and old slaves and caboclos, cigars, sticky ropes of dark tobacco and oily black soap from the West Coast of Africa, drums, rattles, and bells, in short, any of the ritual paraphernalia that one might need, that Jurema is a frequently encountered name for a cabocla (a female caboclo). I would learn also that "jurema" is the common name for a plant, *pithecolobium torta*, an acacia-like tree also known as mimosa. A psychotropic tea, also called jurema, is brewed from its leaves and was traditionally used by diviners and healers in the impoverished, periodically parched backlands of Northeastern Brazil. Many of the inhabitants of the region are of mixed indigenous and African ancestry and are commonly referred to as "caboclos," and all too often by some other, very unflattering, terms. The jurema tea is not generally used in Umbanda, though late one night, at the House of Father John, after almost everyone had left, I did share a little bowl of jurema. It was represented to me as a sacrament, not a drug. I don't know that it "did" anything psychopharmacologically speaking; I do know that sitting there on that dirt floor in the predawn hours, drifting in and out of the streams of soft voices and silent interludes, punctuated by the occasional cock's crow and then by the sudden crescendo of thousands of waking birds, was sublime.

But this night found me standing face-to-face with the cabocla Jurema. Before saying a word, Dona Luciana or, rather, the cabocla Jurema, placed her hand firmly on my heart and looked intently into my eyes. Her look was steely, almost fierce. She then ran her hands up and down my body, from head to toe along the sides, and finally grasped my fingers and pulled down hard. My shoulders bent down and forward and my knees momentarily buckled. Then Jurema spoke. "*O que é que você quer da cabocla Jurema?*" What do you want from the cabocla Jurema? The directness, the brusque tone, the steely gaze, and the aggressive body language seemed to confirm two things. First, my initial impression that Dona Luciana didn't care much for my being there and, second, that caboclos are indeed domineering and arrogant. I felt somewhat rattled and babbled on about not wanting anything except to learn about Umbanda and spirits and caboclos like Jurema. Jurema seemed to soften at this. "What do you want to know? What question do you have for Jurema?" I wanted to know about her life, who she had been. She had been a beautiful young woman, about seventeen, when she died of snakebite in the backlands. Her father had been a very important person, a kind of chief. I asked what tribe she belonged to. Jurema looked at me as though I were a fool. "Tribe? Tribe! I have no tribe! I am a Portuguese girl! A white girl! Do I look like an Indian to you? Do I talk like an Indian? Jurema is no Indian!"

And neither were any of the caboclos who appeared that night at Dona Luciana's apartment. Ronaldo's caboclo, who went by the Indian name of Arranca Toco (Stump Puller), connoting strength and stamina, on further acquaintance turned out to be a mariner from ancient Greece named Hector. Very early in the session, Ronaldo sang a hymn inviting Rompe Mata (Trail Blazer) to descend. He did, and, incorporated in Dona Luciana, came charging out of the bedroom, swinging a sword that he poked into every corner of the apartment to secure the grounds from bad spirits. New as I was at this, I thought Rompe Mata to be one strange Indian indeed when he then performed a kind of knighting ceremony, tapping each of us in turn on the forehead, shoulders, and back with his sword. I would learn that Trail Blazer was actually a Spanish Crusader by the name of Senhor Hernán de la Arena. His departure was followed by the arrival of another caboclo, who I was later told was a French priest who catechized among the Tupi Indians in the interior, several centuries ago. The Indians whose souls he saved loved him but, unfortunately, renegades got hold of him, killed him, and devoured his body. Another cabocla there at Dona Luciana's, who I never met but Dona Luciana told me about, was a Bedouin woman. Dona Luciana rarely receives her, probably just as well, because whenever she does her legs ache the next day as a reminder of the cabocla's endless wanderings through the desert with her possessions on her back. At the House of Father John, most of the caboclos are Indians, but a few of them are cowboys. And in parts of the Northeast, some caboclos are said to be the spirits of Turkish kings. Nonetheless, most caboclos are represented as the spirits of Amazonian Indians, just as Diana Brown stated.

Beginning with that first introduction to the Jurema who was really a young Portuguese woman, I have often asked myself what the caboclos are, what they represent, and what purposes they serve in Umbanda. Obviously, "unacculturated Indians, inhabitants of the Amazonian forests," while true in most cases, is not always true and, in any event, does not take us very far toward addressing these questions. Fortunately, Diana Brown goes on to give valuable insight, as does the legendary French sociologist and expert on African religions in Brazil, Roger Bastide.[3] I draw from both of them, while focusing on the caboclos I have come to know in my field research, as I try to make sense of the caboclos. I suggest that we look at caboclos from four interrelated perspectives: as mediators and symbols of nature; as vehicles for representing and mediating the orixás; as representations of a mythic Brazilian identity; and, finally, as signs of and for the embattled self.

CABOCLOS IN NATURE

In contrast to the old slaves, whose lives of suffering and oppression are largely played out in the stifling, man-made environments of the slave quarters, the plantation fields, or the manor house, the caboclos roam the free, wild spaces. For most, these are the Amazon forests but, as we have seen, they also include the Arabian deserts, the open seas, and the vast backlands where the cowboys tend their herds.

While these are free and wild spaces, these natural spaces are fraught with danger. Jurema, for example told me that she had died of snakebite, and, indeed, caboclo songs and caboclo names frequently allude to dangerous snakes—*Cobra Coral, Sucuri, Jiboia* (Coral Snake, Anaconda, Boa Constrictor). Jaguars stalk the Amazon forests and the cowboy's backlands, and the rivers are infested with crocodiles and piranha. Sandstorms, heat, and thirst rule the deserts, and shipwreck awaits sailors like Hector. As Diana Brown points out, the caboclos are vigorous, at the height of their powers—they must be to survive, and, in fact, dangerous nature generally does them in before age can diminish their strength.[4] And yet the caboclos face these dangers bravely, even with the arrogance Diana Brown alludes to. For example, I am looking right now at a statue I bought depicting the cowboy caboclo known as the *boiadeiro*. Shirtless, clad in a leather vest, hat, and pants, a bolo slung over his shoulder, he leans back against a Brahma bull in a daredevil stance, his face the picture of nonchalance. (A similar statue that I almost bought depicted the bull as nearly seven feet tall, if taken to scale; I passed on it because the animal was a lurid shade of purple). Another statue I bought, this one of a cabocla, portrays a lovely young woman, bare breasted, wearing a feather headdress and a short leather skirt, a jaguar cub at her feet, cradling the head and tail of a very large snake in her two arms. And a few songs I heard told of caboclos wearing coral snakes as belts. Besides a certain arrogance, these images suggest both a supreme confidence and a superb competence and control within their natural world; they are, in that sense, the opposite of the old slaves, who are broken in spirit and largely at the mercy of a cultural world beyond their control.

Though inherently dangerous, the natural world that the caboclos inhabit is portrayed as beautiful, fantastic, supernatural, a place where the natural and the mythical are juxtaposed. This comes through most clearly in the songs that are sung to summon and dismiss the caboclos. That first night I met Jurema, for instance, one of the songs preceding her appearance depicted her as a mermaid who guides sailors and who comes from the snows and the waves of the sea. A song from the House of Father John, again sung when the caboclos are called on, paints a fantastic image of an anaconda and a boa constrictor slithering along the seashore. The natural world of the caboclos regularly departs from ordinary reality, suggesting the supernatural. For example, the song used to call on the French priest (who, by the way, appeared at every caboclo session I attended at Dona Luciana's, making the sign of the cross, sprinkling holy water on all the visitors, and serving a simple communion of bread scraps with water) paints the following picture:

eu vi chover	I saw it rain
e vi relampiar	and saw lightning flash
mas mesmo assim	but even so
o céu estava azul.	the sky was blue
firme seu ponto	sign your "ponto"[5]
nas folhas da Jurema,	in the leaves of the Jurema [tree]
Oxossi reina,	Oxossi[6] reigns
de norte á sul.	from north to south.

Another song, this one from the House of Father John, is used to send the caboclos on their way after they have done their work and suggests a similarly contradictory set of conditions in the sky:

No céu azul	In the blue sky
vi estrela brilhar	I saw a star shine
O! céu azul	O! Blue sky
É a morada de Oxalá	[that] is the home of Oxalá
O galo já cantou	The cock already crowed
á chegada da aurora	at the crack of dawn
o caboclo trabalhou	the caboclo did his work
e ele vai embora	and now he goes away

Stars that shine after the break of day, thunderbolts and rain from a blue sky, mermaids and charmed snakes and jaguar kittens; the caboclos reside in nature, but their effect is to transfigure nature, to make of it or reveal it as supernatural, to enchant it.

CABOCLOS AND ORIXÁS

Below are the words to the song that calls Dona Luciana's Jurema. When I think about the song, listen to it in my mind, I wish that I had learned to read and write music, but I didn't, so I can't convey to those of you who did the wonderful melodies and shifting, sifting rhythms of the song. The best I can do is to tell you that, to me, it evokes the sound and soul of the Portuguese *fado*—romantic, haunting, mysterious.

Salve a cabocla Jurema	Hail the cabocla Jurema
Salve a cabocla do mar	Hail the cabocla of the sea
(bis)	(bis)
com seu arpão na mão	with her harpoon in her hand
com seu canto de sereia	with her mermaid's song
ela vem aqui á terra trabalhar	she comes here to earth to work
(bis)	(bis)
ela vem aqui á terra trabalhar	she comes here to earth to work
ajudar os seus filhos de fé	to help her children of faith
(bis)	(bis)

cabocla Jurema,	cabocla Jurema,
ela vem do mar	she comes from the sea
trazendo consigo	bringing with her
as folhas de Iemanjá	the leaves of Iemanjá
(bis)	(bis)
ela já chegou	she has already arrived
das ondas do mar	from the waves of the sea
trazendo consigo	bringing with her
as forças de Iemanjá	the powers of Iemanjá

The song implicitly equates the sea and the astral, from where spirits come to help their children of faith, but it is a sea enchanted, inhabited by mermaids whose songs guide sailors to safety or to shipwreck. The song explicitly identifies Jurema as the servant of Iemanjá—it is she who brings with her the leaves and the powers of the goddess while implicitly identifying Jurema with Iemanjá, both inhabiting the enchanted sea. Sometimes the identification is more explicit; often, not always, the repeated second line is changed a little, becoming *Salve a rainha do mar*, that is, "Hail the *queen* of the sea," the queen being the goddess Iemanjá.

As with the old slaves, the caboclos are called on to help people with all kinds of problems; as occurred during the session in which I first encountered Jurema, much or most of their time is spent giving passes, listening to problems, giving advice, and proffering spiritual assistance. Beyond that, though, the caboclos represent the orixás, bringing their presence and, as the song suggests, their powers to the earthly settings of Umbanda centers. There are reasons why this must be done, why caboclos are mainly responsible for doing it, and various ways in which this presence and power are represented.

In Umbanda centers, the actual orixás rarely appear. Even at the House of Father John, the orixás as orixás mainly appear during special rituals, coinciding with their saints' days or with the initiation or reconfirmation of one their "children," as described in this volume's chapter on orixás. Even then, a number of participants were keen to point out that this practice was "Candomblé," as distinct from Umbanda. All other times, the orixás are represented by various caboclos.

Dona Luciana, along with numerous others, identifies three main reasons for this absence of orixás. The orixás are occupied with larger spiritual matters. The orixás are too powerful and awesome for us; their presence would be dangerous. And, as vibrations and forces of nature, the orixás are of such a different order of being that their presence would be beyond our comprehension. Thus they send instead their delegated representatives, the caboclos. The caboclos willingly give of their time; they are powerful, but not dangerously so; and being disincarnated persons, they are enough like us that they understand us, and we them. Thus, in that session back in 1986 when I first met Jurema, Ogum, the god of war and iron and agriculture came first, represented by his servant, Senhor Hernán de la Arena; then came the French priest, envoy of Oxossi the Hunter; and, finally, Jurema, cabocla of the sea and daughter of Iemanjá.

While the old slaves, like the caboclos, serve the orixás, it is the caboclos and not the old slaves who personify or represent them. The reasons are rooted in the myths of Brazilian identity and history. Although we have seen that the old slaves can indeed represent resistance, their stories are stories of defeat and subjugation. The Indians, on the other hand, represent defiance, an unbending will to remain free; they may die fighting, but they do not die in captivity[7] (of course, this is the myth, not necessarily historical reality). They are fierce, untamed, yet noble; in the Brazilian mythos, as in the North American one, the noble savage is a key figure. Unbroken, supremely confident and competent, even arrogant; vigorous; at home in the vast wilderness; how could the caboclos *not* be the vehicles bringing the presence and the power of the orixás, often called the "forces of nature," to Umbanda?

If the orixás are forces, vibrations, mysteries, the caboclos, when not doing the everyday work of helping people with their problems, can be seen as metaphors through which Umbandistas experientially grasp these mysterious, forceful vibrations. At the House of Father John, this is done mainly through dance. As the drummers pound out the rhythms for the various orixás in turn, mediums receive caboclos representing those orixás, and those caboclos dance the distinctive dances of those orixás. The mysterious, forceful vibration is rendered as kinesthetic metaphor.

At Dona Luciana's, the primary media were not dance but rather song and Dona Luciana's thespian performances. The song that calls Senhor Hernán de la Arena, representative of Ogum, god of war, combines a stirring melody and forceful, upbeat tempo, the bright imagery of daybreak and seashore and a charging stallion, and the mythos of crusaders and knights in the service of the Blessed Virgin:

Rompe-Mata é cavalheiro de Oxalá	Rompe Mata is a knight of Oxalá
e ordinança da Virgem Maria	and soldier of the Virgin Mary
(bis)	(bis)
ele vem em seu cavalo	he comes on his horse
ao romper da aurora	at the crack of dawn
ao raiar o dia	at the break of day
(bis)	(bis)
eu vi raiar do dia	I saw the break of day
eu vi estrela brilhar	I saw a star shine
eu vi seu Rompe Mata,	I saw Rompe Mata,
Ogum das matas passear,	Ogum of the forests passing
á beira mar	by the seashore

And Dona Luciana, in the character of Senhor Hernan de la Arena, sword in hand, moves with force and vigor, the face at once fierce and cheerful. The mysterious vibration becomes a figure of ruddy strength, a stirring song, a robust embrace, a mood; a caboclo one can see and touch.

And then Oxossi comes. The song, slow and minor key, uses equally clear, evocative visual imagery to set an entirely different mood:

A mata estava escura	The forest was dark
veio luar, e clareou	the moonlight came, and it grew light
ouviu-se a voz do senhor	the voice of the Lord was heard
é seu Oxossi que aqui chegou	it is Oxossi who arrived here
ele é o rei,	he is the king
ele é o rei, ele é o rei	he is the king, he is the king
ele é o rei,	he is the king
na Aruanda ele é o rei	in Aruanda he is the king

And Dona Luciana, as the French Priest who represents Oxossi, moves with a light, slow grace that suggests a very different mystery and vibration than that of Ogum. Ogum charges forth; this Oxossi you would not hear as he glides through the forest. And then, finally, comes Jurema.

The specific performances I sketched above are particular to Dona Luciana's. At other places, different caboclos behaving in different ways appear, "bringing the forces" and representing the orixás in their own ways. In common to all, the caboclos are, though, the allegories, the visible, embodied, moving metaphors through which the orixás appear in Umbanda.

CABOCLOS AND MYTHICAL IDENTITY

Brazilians, one hears over and over, are a miscegenized people, a mixture of European, African, and Indian. A drop of white, a drop of black, a drop of red, as I mentioned previously. The panoply of Umbanda spirits reflects this ancestry and comments upon its meanings. Many of the exus and pomba-giras (though by no means all) are portrayed as white and certainly the history, mythical and real, of Europeans and their descendents, the owners of slaves, killers of Indians, oppressors of peasants, and captains of industry (and at the same time the bearers of "civilized" culture) match the exus' moral ambiguity, guilt, and potency. The old slaves as symbols of Afro-Brazilians, their sufferings and strengths, past and present, I have already discussed.

The caboclos, clearly, represent the indigenous contribution to this mythical, miscegenized identity (though not, as we have seen, in the case of Dona Luciana's Jurema and Senhor de la Arena). Clearly, however, there is more to this than meets the eye.

First, the representations of caboclos is thoroughly permeated by stereotypical notions of indigenous peoples. Indigenous peoples have always been negatively stereotyped in Brazil, but beginning in the nineteenth century a kind of counter discourse of positive stereotypes has been available. Nineteenth-century novelists, most notably José de Alencar, portrayed the Indians as noble savages—brave warriors, trusted servants, beautiful princesses, heroic men and women. These, it seems clear to me, are the models for most of the caboclo spirits.[8]

Second, the caboclos must be understood not in isolation but in contrast to the old slaves. As Roger Bastide suggests, the national mythology has it that the Indians resisted domination, dying for their freedom or retreating back into the forests, while the blacks submitted to slavery and adopted a strategy of accommodation, an ethos of humility, meekness, and forgiveness. For the poor and disenfranchised, and there are many of those in Umbanda, the old slaves represent the latter strategy, while the caboclos, Bastide suggests, allow Umbandistas to assume, at least in ritual, the pride, potency, and autonomy of the mythical Indian.

CABOCLOS AS SIGNS OF AND FOR THE SELF

Despite its somewhat rocky beginning, my first interview with Jurema turned out quite well. Overcoming her initial indignation at my presumptuous preconceptions, Jurema went on to sketch out her life history. She had been born centuries ago, during the colonial period in Portugal, to an aristocratic family. Her father was an important figure at the Court. The king, concerned with revenues and rumors of malfeasance in the diamond mines, charged Jurema's father to investigate, audit, and report. Jurema, then a young woman of perhaps seventeen years, begged to accompany him on the long, arduous journey to the diamond region of Minas Gerais.

A fatal plea, as it turned out; somewhere in the backlands of Brazil, a snake bit Jurema and she succumbed to its venom. Jurema's voice turned soft; her eyes far away and misty, she paused for several seconds to compose herself. She turned to Ronaldo, beckoning him from the far corner of the room. "Listen, my son," she said to him, her voice once again short and gruff, "after I leave, you tell my 'horse' [medium, i.e., Dona Luciana] that this traveler [poking me in the heart with the flat of her hand] is good. She is to make him welcome here."

And Dona Luciana did make me welcome. Not only to attend sessions every week, but to talk for hours after sessions and at other times about all kinds of things. Her upbringing, the day-to-day and the momentous events she had lived through during most of a tumultuous century of Brazilian history, her bemused, ambivalent feelings about the present moment of Brazilian culture and society. And, of course, we talked a lot about Umbanda, the cosmos, and spirits. Dona Luciana had some interesting stories to tell about Jurema, who, it turned out, is a vivid presence in Dona Luciana's life, and not only during those weekly Umbanda sessions where she healed and advised and sometimes enlightened her visitors. "Jurema," Dona Luciana told me, "is my guide, my guardian angel." Jurema advises her; sometimes, as we saw above, by giving a medium or a visitor a message to give to Dona Luciana later; sometimes, more simply, more directly, by leaving thoughts and intuitions in Dona Luciana's consciousness as she sleeps or watches television late at night. Jurema protects Dona Luciana, stepping in at dangerous moments; she corrects Dona Luciana when she strays from the path. Sometimes, Jurema's communiqués are phrased in extended drama. The following episode of spiritual pedagogy, occurring early in Dona Luciana's career as a medium, took seven years to unfold:

It seems at that time Ronaldo's father (Luciana's brother), who worked at the Naval Station, was undergoing some difficult financial circumstances. Always one of her favorites, Dona Luciana offers to help him out by lending him a bracelet her mother had left her that he could pawn until payday (following her separation from her husband, Dona Luciana is not in a position to just loan or give him the money). That way he could pay his bills. He pawns the bracelet. Payday arrives, he can't get away from work, and so he calls Dona Luciana. He tells her to leave early for her Umbanda session that night, drop by the house on the way, pick up a big leather purse from his wife (the money and the pawn ticket would be in the purse), and drop by the bank to redeem the bracelet.[9] Easy enough.

Dona Luciana gets the purse. The bank is on the way to the Umbanda center, which is on the other side of town. But Dona Luciana is running late and decides to put off redeeming the pawn until the next day. The bus is very crowded, and Dona Luciana is standing with the purse over her shoulder and her bag full of Umbanda clothes and gear in her arms. She feels something cold against her ribs—who knows what in that crush of people?—and then suddenly people are talking to her. "Did he get anything?" "Are you okay?" "He had a gun!" Dona Luciana emerges from her confusion, looks down, and sees the purse is slit. Witnesses tell her that the thief had a gun stuck in her ribs the whole time. The money gone, the pawn ticket gone, and gone, too, maybe, the most treasured memento she has from her mother. The thief might already have it—he would only need the pawn ticket and the money, and the bracelet was worth much more than that. Even if the thief chose not to take the risk of passing the stolen ticket, how could Dona Luciana redeem the pawn with no money and no ticket? In desperation, Dona Luciana called on Jurema and made a promise, right there: "Help me get it back, Jurema, and I will give you seven white roses on the beach before I do anything else."

Jurema does her part. Dona Luciana calls the bank; the man who handled the pawn answers the phone, and, yes, he certainly remembers her brother and would make sure the bracelet remained at the bank—at least for a reasonable time, but eventually they would have to sell it. Back home the next day, bits and dabs of money come in—gifts, repayments on small loans to friends, and so on—more than enough money. Dona Luciana gets on the bus, goes downtown, redeems the bracelet, and returns home, determined to go to the beach at the crack of dawn to make her offering to Jurema. Dona Luciana clasps the bracelet on her wrist—all is well with the world.

But she meets up with a friend. It's a beautiful, sunny day and her friend wants to go to the beach. Dona Luciana declines—she promised to make the offering before she did anything else. But her friend talks her into it. Dona Luciana walks out into the surf. Kerplonk! The bracelet falls off. She retrieves it, puts it on, and makes extra sure the clasp is closed. Kerplonk! It falls off again. And then again. Shaken, Dona Luciana tells her friend she must leave and, bracelet in hand, goes off to buy seven white roses.

Dona Luciana is very discreet about making offerings or doing anything to reveal her Umbanda practice to strangers. That is part of why she had planned to make the offering at daybreak; there would be no one around. And dawn is an auspicious time. But this is urgent. Carrying the roses, candles, and the bracelet, she returns to the crowded beach and makes the offering. She hears Jurema telling her to put on the bracelet, and she does. All is settled, or so she thinks. But then she goes to remove the bracelet that evening—and it won't come off. The clasp that wouldn't hold earlier now will not let go. She goes to a jeweler. He tells her the only way to get it off would be to cut it off. Dona Luciana wears the bracelet for seven years. Then one night Ronaldo is sleeping over, sharing her bed, her head at his feet and his head at hers ("So I could kick him when he snores!") Suddenly Dona Luciana wakes up. Ronaldo is sitting bolt straight. He later reports having seen at that moment a woman standing above the bed. Dona Luciana and Ronaldo hear Jurema's voice: "*Chegou a hora*" (The time has come). The bracelet falls from Dona Luciana's wrist.

Dona Luciana refers to this episode as a *prova*, which means both test and proof. Tested and proven are both Dona Luciana and Jurema. Tests and proofs are predicated on truth, on finding it, demonstrating it (or demonstrating its lack), convincing oneself or others of it. A number of truths are revealed in this prova, some obvious. Jurema is a formidable ally. On the bus, Dona Luciana comes to no harm, though a thief pokes a gun in her ribs. Jurema didn't let her even notice—"imagine if I would have known, and panicked: I could have been killed!" (As Dona Luciana invariably points out, wide-eyed, jaw dropped, when telling this story. "Imagine!"). Jurema arranges events—oh, certainly, it could be interpreted as coincidence, though not by Dona Luciana—so that Dona Luciana reclaims her mother's legacy. If the story proves the efficacy of Jurema, it underlines also the peril of slighting her. It even proves that Jurema is real: Ronaldo saw her.

Not so obviously, perhaps, it is an extended testing and eventual proving of Dona Luciana. It is a story of coming up short and, eventually, through Jurema's guidance, overcoming. At the beginning of the story Dona Luciana is weak, irresponsible, someone who plays frivolously with things of great worth. She fails a test of judgment: she risks the one important gift she had left from her mother on a pawn to pay a few bills. Surely in her large and connected family, there were alternatives? She fails to keep her promise to Jurema. And then she fails to respect Jurema's disposition of the matter, instead seeking a jeweler to free herself from the bracelet. But then she submits, enduring the bracelet for seven years. During those seven years, Dona Luciana grew and grew in Umbanda, achieving mastery over herself as she worked hard at helping others, all the time guided and protected and informed by Jurema, whose presence is symbolically marked by the bracelet. The gift that she almost frittered away and then couldn't possess, and then couldn't get away from, becomes hers to take on and put off at will. The reader can interpret this metaphor for herself.

Jurema, it seems, guarded and guided Dona Luciana well. She passed her test.

Setting aside for a moment Jurema's role as guide and guardian of Dona Luciana, it is striking that Jurema, the young woman from Portugal, is one of a cohort of caboclos of European descent that appear during sessions at Dona Luciana's: the Spanish crusader, Hernán de la Arena; Hector the

Greek Sailor; the French Priest. While there are others, Indian caboclos who appear occasionally (for example, Jureminha, a little Indian princess) these are the main ones, and they are European. At all other centers I visited, European caboclos were either rare or simply not there at all. Beyond that, Dona Luciana's pomba-gira, Mari-Carmen, hails from Andalusia.

I would suggest that in this constellation of European entities we can read Dona Luciana's own sense of identity. Though born in Brazil, her parents were Portuguese, and she visited the old country many times during her childhood. Unlike most Umbandistas, she does not see herself in terms of the Brazilian myth of the mixture of three races—European, Indian, and African. She sees herself as European by ancestry. If at some level spirits are signs of and for the self, figures that speak to the dramas of each medium's existence, then Dona Luciana's mainly European cast of characters makes a certain kind of sense.

In Jurema we can read an allegorical biography. Again let me turn to a conversation with Dona Luciana, again in regard to Jurema.

The moment when Jurema arrives is both striking and telling. Caboclos typically announce their arrival by letting out a war cry, a whoop, a *grito*, that, in the popular idioms of movies and children's play, signals "Indian." Jurema's grito is very different; it is her mermaid's song. It is a remarkable performance. The first split second sounds like the "war cry" a child makes by bouncing the palm over the open, vocalizing mouth. But that is over so immediately as to go almost unnoticed as the sound modulates into a wordless melody spread over a considerable range of pitch and volume. The sound is rich, liquid, silvery, and full of vibrato and color. It is the kind of sound that comes out of a singer who is unusually gifted, trained, and in good form. Listeners marvel at the fact that the singer is a small and elderly woman in less than robust health.

One evening Dona Luciana and I were talking about Jurema, when we got on the subject of Jurema's song. I told her that it was a fantastic thing, that amazing voice coming out of her body. How is it possible? Dona Luciana seemed to not understand my puzzlement. She had heard

that Jurema's song was impressive but, being the kind of medium who
has no conscious awareness when in trance, she had no firsthand knowledge of Jurema's incredible vocal performance. She had never heard the
mermaid sing.

So I asked Dona Luciana if she would like to hear a tape of Jurema. I
had recorded Jurema during a session and that evening played it back for
Dona Luciana. She was astonished. On one level, it was another prova, a
proof, a demonstration, of Jurema's power that she could bring that kind
of sound out of Dona Luciana's small, elderly body—she understood
my earlier question now, and the power of Jurema was her answer. On
another level, she was deeply moved by the song itself, which is indeed
for most listeners haunting and compelling and graceful. And, hearing
Jurema revealed, in a very concrete, sensual way, another aspect of this
spirit who is so central to Dona Luciana's life. Dona Luciana was open-
mouthed in wonder.

Dona Luciana speculated aloud. "Jurema must be a trained singer, but
how? Well," Dona Luciana went on, "being the daughter of a high official,
she would have had an education, training in the arts, music—"

My thoughts went back to conversations we had about Dona Luciana's
upbringing. Her parents, from old elite families, had immigrated to Brazil
from Portugal before she was born. As a child and adolescent, Dona
Luciana had studied piano and voice. Jurema died at seventeen, suddenly;
Dona Luciana's youth, one could even say her spirit, died slowly during a
long period of difficult adulthood, but it didn't quite die completely. As
we saw in Chapter 2, Dona Luciana, terribly wounded by the poisoned
bite of that phase of her life, finds her spirits and is in profound ways
redeemed and rejuvenated.

The young Luciana sings, through the Jurema who sings her mermaid's song through the aged body of Dona Luciana.

Orixás

It had been up till then an altogether wonderful day, one of those winter days when the sky is baby blue and crystal clear, the air warm, dry, and sea-breeze scented, the ocean gentle and cool. It was an August day, the day of Our Lady of Glory, who Dona Luciana and many other Umbandistas understand to be an aspect of the sea goddess Iemanjá. And it was in Iemanjá's realm that Dona Luciana and several friends and members of her family were that afternoon—at sea, off the coast several miles from Rio de Janeiro, heading home relaxed and happy after a day of eating and drinking, laughing and playing on the beach of a remote little island. Unnoticed at first, a line of clouds was building off to the south, the soft breezes shifted and took on sharp, cold edges—and then, in the space of a few minutes, the skies blackened, the winds howled, the gentle swells reared up into steep, black water canyons, and the horizon vanished in sheets of driving rain. As the boat tossed and porpoised, Dona Luciana held on tight and prayed on that day of Our Lady of Glory, to her mother; not the flesh and blood mother who bore her, but her spiritual mother, the sea goddess Iemanjá.

Iemanjá, who Dona Luciana calls "my mother Iemanjá," is an orixá. In her *Dicionário de Cultos Afro-Brasileiros* (Dictionary of Afro-Brazilian Cults), Olga Guidolle Cacciatore tells us that orixás, except for the supreme deity Olorun, are intermediary deities, that in Africa there are about six hundred of them, that about fifty were brought over to Brazil, with sixteen celebrated in the traditional Afro-Brazilian Candomblé, and that only nine are found in Umbanda.[1] As she goes on to note, the orixás represent the elemental forces and features of nature, and the primordial economic activities of humankind.

The orixás are dramatic characters in a rich and wonderful mythology, originating in West Africa and remembered and, in some cases, reinvented in Brazil.[2] Like the Greek or Roman gods, the orixás are portrayed in myth as very much like us, driven by desires, emotions, full of wisdom and folly, ego, greed, generosity, rage, tenderness, and love. Each inhabits various aspects of nature—thunder, lightening, the forest, the tempest, the diseases that plague us, the plants that heal us, the flowing streams, and endless seas. They are equally culture heroes, bringers and patrons of law and justice, war, iron, agriculture, hunting, domestic comforts, and more. They are associated with Catholic saints, represented on Umbanda altars in painted plaster images of Our Lady of the Conception, Saint George, Santa Anna, Santa Barbara, Jesus Christ, and Saint Jerome (among others).

Nine orixás figure prominently in both Afro-Brazilian and White Umbanda as I observed it:

(1) Oxalá, the son of Olorun, is the creator of humankind and the beloved king of orixás and people. Oxala's residence is the sky; his color is white, his emblem is a shepherd's staff, and he is kind and pure and good. He is identified (a process I will discuss below) with Jesus Christ. His day is Friday.

(2) Nanã is often described as the mother of all the orixás. Like Iemanjá, Nanã is a water deity, but her waters are the still waters of the lake or the swamp. She is the orixá of rain, and mud, the primeval substance. Nanã is gentle, dignified, calm, and patient; motherly, or perhaps better put, *grandmotherly*; when Nanã incorporates in a medium at the house of Father John, she is led by the hand to a chair and, like an old, old aunt or grandmother, gently helped to her seat. If there is a

baby in the house, it will be placed on her lap; if not, she is given a big bundle of gladiolus and other flowers to cradle in her lap. She is identified with Saint Anne, mother of Mary. Her color is violet. Her day is Tuesday.

(3) Omolu is the orixá of sickness and healing. He wears a straw garment that covers him from head to toe. A story I heard had it that, one day, Omolu, beloved son of Naná, fell ill with fever. Soon he was covered with the pustules of smallpox. His mother could no longer bear the sight of him, so she made a mask of straw to cover his face and body. But eventually the stench of his festering sores became too much even for a mother to bear; she sent him on his way, up the road. He soon encountered a village. The people were entranced with his gorgeous mask and very much in need of his healing powers, so they welcomed him. But soon enough they too began to break out and, attributing this to Omolu's presence, sent him on up the road to the next village, where the cycle repeated itself. And so on and so forth. The age of smallpox is long past, but beginning in the late 1980s Omolu was "reinvented" in many quarters as the patron of those with HIV/AIDS. Omolu's colors are black and white, he is associated with Saint Roch and with Lazarus, and Monday is his day.

(4) Iemanjá is the sea goddess. Like Naná, Iemanjá is sometimes referred to as the mother of all the orixás. In statues and paintings, she is often depicted as a voluptuous, raven haired beauty, dressed in a clinging blue and white robe, a star affixed to her headdress, emerging from the sea. Iemanjá has powerful maternal instincts; indeed, she loves her children so much that sometimes she pulls them under the waves to live with her in her palace at the bottom of the sea. Iemanjá

is associated with Our Lady of Glory. While the twelfth of August is the day of Our Lady of Glory, thousands of followers throng to the beaches of Rio to make offerings to Iemanjá on New Year's Eve. Her colors are light blue, white, and pink. Saturday is her day.

(5) Ogum is the god of war and the patron of metalworking, agriculture, and transportation. Umbanda hymns depict Ogum as a warrior, his banners white, green, and red; he is the general who wins the battle without losing a single soldier, the protector of children of faith. Tuesday is Ogum's day.

(6) Xangô is the god of thunder and justice and the patron of stoneworking. As with the other orixás, a rich mythology surrounds Xangô. Xangô was once a mortal, the king of a city state, and his greatest accomplishment was to implement a system of laws and justice. Not surprisingly, many of his people grew tired of these restraints, and they eventually dethroned Xangô, who wandered off dejected into the woods. Devastated, Xangô hung himself by an iron chain from a tree. The chain broke, and Xangô's body struck the earth with such force as to bury itself, leaving only the end of his chain above ground. The people by this time had realized the wisdom of Xangô's laws and regretted their treatment of him. They went out in search of him and found the chain and his corpse. The orixás were so moved by their pleas, and by Xangô's sacrifice, that they resurrected him and gave him eternal life and supernatural powers. He is represented holding a double edged hatchet, indicating that justice cuts both ways, friend and foe alike. He is associated with Saint Jerome and, like Saint Jerome, who is depicted seated with a lion at his feet, Xangô exudes a stately, majestic power. Maroon is his color, Wednesday his day.

(7) Oxum is the goddess of fertility. Like Naná and Iemanjá, she is associated with water, in her case the flowing fresh waters of streams and, especially, waterfalls. Beautiful, motherly, seductive, and sensual, her color is blue, and her day is Saturday.

(8) Iansá manifests in the tempest and other violent storms. She is a warrior, and mythology depicts her as fiercely independent, aggressive, and sexual. Married to Xangô, myths attest to numerous affairs. She alone among orixás has no fear of the dead; with her horsetail whisk, she drives and dominates the souls of the deceased, sweeping them before her on the path to Aruanda. Like Xangô, her day is Wednesday. She is associated with Saint Barbara, and coral is her color.

(9) Oxossi is Ogum's younger brother. He is the great hunter and inhabits the forest. His color is green, his day Thursday, and he is associated with Saint Sebastian.

In addition, there are three orixás that are an important presence in what I have called the Afro-Brazilian Umbanda practiced at the House of Father John, but absent entirely from the White Umbanda of Dona Luciana and the House of Saint Benedict. They are:

(1) Oxumaré, the rainbow serpent, symbol of eternal renewal and youth, like the snake who sheds his old dead skin to become shiny and new again. Oxumaré is sometimes depicted as a snake devouring its own tail, in an endless cycle of life and death. Oxumaré is bisexual, female part of the year, male the other part. Oxumaré's colors are yellow and green, his/her day is Tuesday, and he/she is associated with Saint Bartholomew.

(2) Ossaim, the divinity of sacred and medicinal plants. His day is Saturday, his colors green and white, and he is associated with Saint Benedict.

(3) Tempo, also known as Loko or Iroko. "Tempo" in Portuguese means time and weather. Tempo is associated with Saint Lawrence, who was martyred on an iron grill over an open fire. His colors are various, though white, green, and brown are most common. Some informants told me that Thursday is his day, while others had no opinion.

I will have more to say further on about Oxumaré, Ossaim, and Tempo, and why they figure so prominently at the House of Father John and not at all in the White Umbanda of Dona Luciana and the House of Saint Benedict.

Returning to the events of the day of Our Lady of Glory that we opened this chapter with, Iemanjá was angry. Iemanjá had given so much to Dona Luciana—protection, strength, tranquility, insight—and yet Dona Luciana had neglected to do the little things she asked in return, Dona Luciana could not be bothered to walk down to the beach on the morning of Our Lady of Glory to do her annual obligation to Iemanjá: to light a candle and wade out into the surf to offer her mother a wooden tray piled with offerings of flowers, fruit, champagne, and fish? Instead Dona Luciana set aside her promise and went running off on a boat to eat and drink and party on the day of Iemanjá. Let the wind howl and the sea boil; let Dona Luciana learn the meaning of respect.

As the wind and the waves and the rain pounded the boat, Dona Luciana pleaded with her mother Iemanjá. "Forgive me. Punish me, but these others are not to blame; let them live. Let us live; I promise, the hour we set foot on land, I will meet my obligation. I'll never forget again. Forgive me."

According to Dona Luciana, every one of us is endowed with a *coroa*, that is, a crown, consisting of the spiritual entities that engender, shape, and protect us. These include a guardian angel—in Dona Luciana's coroa, this is her cabocla spirit Jurema—an exu or pomba-gira, and, very importantly, the orixás. These entities are arranged hierarchically, and everyone's coroa is unique in terms of its components and their order, but the most important entity is an orixá known as the *orixá da frente*, the "front" or lead orixá, though, suggestively perhaps, "frente" can also mean the forehead. Following the lead orixá is the second orixá, the third, and so forth. All are part of who we are and the fate we live out, but the first two are especially important and Dona Luciana, like most Umbandistas, talks about them within the idiom of kinship. Her orixá da frente, Iemanjá, she refers to as her mother, while Ogum, her second, is her spiritual father.[3]

Just as a person's physical and, to some extent, psychological characteristics are in part inherited from the biological parents, a person's spiritual and, to some extent, psychological and character traits are derived from the orixá "parents." For example, Ogum is (among other things) optimistic, brave, generous, but capable of terrible violence; Iemanjá is willful, protective, maternal, concerned with others, sometimes arrogant, easily offended, and demanding. And each of the other orixás is likewise a rich mixture of traits. With each person being a blend of the traits of two rather complex personages, this folk psychology constitutes a rich metaphoric system for understanding and talking about persons and personalities.

The system is enriched further by the fact that each orixá occurs in multiple qualities or forms—there is not just one Oxum, or one Ogum, but many, and each is distinct. The multiplicity is suggested by mythology. For example, there are nine Iansás and seven Ogums. The story is that Iansá and Ogum were once lovers. Ogum possessed an iron rod that, were he to strike a man with it, would break the man in seven parts; it would break a woman in nine. Ogum forged another such rod for his warrior lover. Iansá soon enough tired of Ogum (Ogum is notoriously unlucky in love) and took up with Xangô. Enraged, Ogum chased them down and went after Iansã with his iron rod. Iansã raised her rod, and they both struck simultaneously. Thus seven Ogums and nine Iansãs. And though each follows the basic pattern of Ogum or Iansã, each is distinct. The same holds for the variant forms of the other orixás. There is for example an old Oxalá, full of the wisdom and patience and suffering of the aged; there is a young Oxalá bursting with energy and glowing with the sweetness and innocence of a child. And so forth. There are, in short, mothers and fathers for every variety of person.

Knowing one's spiritual parents can lead to profound insights into the self, into recognizing and making sense of one's strengths and weakness, one's temperament and tendencies. The orixás in turn constitute models for the ongoing construction of the self; Professor Monique Augras, a psychologist, suggests that persons who know which are their orixás become more like them over time.[4] And knowing who others' spiritual parents are gives important insights into their quirks and character (and encourages acceptance; for example, Teresa's quick temper, pushiness, and proclivity for amorous adventures is her Iansã coming out; João's tendency to wallow in suffering comes from his father Omolu; they are as they are, as they should be). As important an insight, maybe more important, is that one's orixás are one's protectors and patrons; by treating them well—making offerings, celebrating their anniversaries, keeping them in one's heart—life goes better and, not only that, the orixás are *owed* that appreciation. It is not good if they feel slighted. So it is important to know one's orixás.

There are a few ways to determine who one's orixá da frente, second, and the rest are. In Candomblé, this is done through divination. A devotee of *Ifá*, the orixá of divination, interprets the patterns cast by successive throws of cowry shells. All kinds of matters are clarified through this technique, among them the question of one's spiritual parentage. This divinatory technique, the *dilogun*, is ancient, and it is an essential part of Candomblé, but it is not used in Umbanda, at least not among any of the groups I worked with. In Umbanda, the determination is usually made by a medium. Some mediums, such as Dona Luciana, possess *vidéncia*, or "seeing." Sometimes Dona Luciana actually sees the entities hovering around; more often, she sees their auras. A sensitive medium, not possessed of vidéncia, will rely on intuition; he or she just "knows." A trusted caboclo or an old slave spirit can also make the determination.

Dona Luciana relied on her vidéncia to determine my orixás. So did Seu Silva, at the House of Father John. Seu Gomes's old slave spirit Mané (he of the UFO tales, the Planet Cabal, and Atlantis) weighed in, as did Seu Silva's caboclo Golden Mountain and Dona Luciana's cabocla Jurema and her old slave Father Gerônimo. A number of other mediums and spirits checked in as well. The verdict was unanimous: Ogum is your father, your orixá da frente; and Oxum is your mother.

The orixás, as I suggested earlier, are associated with various Catholic saints. The particular saint that an orixá is associated with varies somewhat, depending mainly on region. In Rio, for example, Iemanjá is typically associated with Our Lady of Glory, while in Salvador, Bahia, considered the "Rome" of Candomblé, she is usually paired with Our Lady of the Conception, who in Rio is identified with Oxum, the goddess of fertility. Ogum is Saint George in Rio, but in Bahia he is associated with Saint Anthony (as he is throughout the Northeast), no doubt in part because Saint Anthony is a military figure in Bahia—indeed, Saint Anthony was given an officer's commission in a number of army regiments in the Northeast.[5] At the House of Father John, Ogum is both Saint George and Saint Anthony. This reflects the strong influence of Candomblé at the House of Father John, as well as Seu Silva's identification with his *nordestino* (northeastern) roots.

The nature of these associations or identifications is complex and controversial. Dona Luciana, for example, rejected the simple notion that the saint and the orixá are the same—that Ogum and Saint George are one. In her view, Saint George is a manifestation of Ogum. Or rather, Ogum and Saint George are manifestations of the same spirit, entities vibrating to the same frequency, composed as it were of the same spiritual substance—related, but distinct. Most people I discussed this with gave a similar account, some also invoking the notion that the saints are historical incarnations of the orixás, in the same way, for example, as Jesus would be the historical incarnation of the spiritual entity known as God (or Oxalá).

But others take different views. Some years back the renowned and revered Candomblé mãe de santo, Mãe Menininha, led a number of her colleagues in denouncing the association of Catholic saints with orixás and removing images and references to the saints from their terreiros. In their view, the "syncretism" of saints and orixás was an artifact of slavery and oppression and degraded and mystified the truth of the orixás. Catholicism is one thing, Candomblé another, and to mix the two is to disrespect both, the argument went. To exorcize the saints is, in this view, to reclaim truth and clarity and claim liberation.[6]

Roberto, a young medium at the House of Father John, was quite explicit on this point. "*Santo é santo, Orixá é Orixá; Orixá não tem nada a ver com santo*" (Saint is saint, orixá is orixá; orixá has nothing to do with saint). Others at the House of Father John offered a thoroughly pragmatic explanation for the syncretism of saints and orixás: during slavery, the masters and the priests tried to suppress African religion. For instance, they would destroy the *assentamentos*, the clay jars containing the sacred items that both represented and housed the orixás. But the slaves found ways to outfox the masters and the priests. In the slave quarters, they would make an altar out of a table, draping a sheet of cloth over it and placing on it the images of Jesus and the various saints and Our Ladies. The master would look in and see this obvious sign of devotion to the Catholic faith. Souls saved! But underneath the table, behind the cloth, were those clay jars representing the orixás. Those candles burning for Saint Barbara and Saint Anthony and Jesus: they were really for Iansã and Ogum and Oxalá. The saint become associated with the orixá whose assentamento resided underneath his or her feet. Strictly arbitrary, or so the story goes.

I asked Roberto then, if saint and orixá are strictly separate, why it is that the statues of the saints remain at the House of Father John, and why do so many of the songs that call and praise the orixás explicitly associate the orixás with specific saints? The orixás, he said, are vibrations, forces of nature, cosmic principles, and such things are abstract, difficult to grasp, hard to relate to at an emotional level. The images of saints, though—Saint George on his white charger, slaying the dragon at his feet; bare-chested Saint Jerome seated on the rock with his scroll, one hand resting on the head of a sleeping lion—are familiar, vivid, and concrete. They help our limited minds to "visualize" the orixá. They are just visual aids, but too many people, according to Roberto, mistake the image for the orixá.

Roberto's comment, that the image helps us to "visualize" the orixá, suggests that the relationship between the two is one of metaphor. In a metaphor, two terms are related in an implicit comparison in order to represent, make salient, and elucidate the nature of one of the terms.[7] The latter term is, like the orixá, the mystery; the term to which it is compared is typically something more familiar, concrete, often more sensually present and vivid—such as Saint George the dragon slayer. The qualities of the familiar term in some way evoke, echo, and illuminate the qualities in the mysterious term, suggesting they are somehow alike. Saint George on his charger is not Ogum but, as a metaphor, he suggests Ogum's courage, vigor, and fight. Similarly, the other associations of orixá and saint involve resemblance and metaphor. Iansá is the fearless warrior princess. Saint Barbara is martyred by her own father for her Christian faith—as he beheads her, lightening flashes from her neck (as lightening flashes from the tempest cloud) and strikes him dead—Iansá would approve. Omolu is the smallpox, and now AIDS, sufferer, shunned and marginalized; Saint Roch is the plague victim, cast out with only his little dog to bring him bread. The saints, from this perspective, are useful for thinking about the orixás because they represent them through the poetic logic of metaphor.

While Roberto's comments suggest that the Catholic saints are employed as metaphors, as aids in visualizing and grasping the African deities, comments that I heard from numerous Umbandistas (Roberto included) suggest that the mythical personages—Ogum the warrior, Oxum the beautiful mother—are themselves metaphors, that the orixás are in reality not beings but forces, vibrations, qualities, mysteries that we personify in our attempts to grasp that which is beyond our understanding, to feel closeness and kinship with the awesome, inhuman forces that comprise the universe.

The vividness, emotional depth, intimacy, imaginative shape, and narrative structure that metaphor lends to experience is illustrated quite poignantly when we refer back to events of Dona Luciana's day of Our Lady of Glory, as she prays to Iemanjá in the midst of the sudden violent storm: "Forgive me. I promise." As she tells it, the prayer echoed in her heart, filling her being to overflowing. And as it flowed out, the winds howled less and less, the driving rain slowed, the sea calmed, the sky lightened. The boat made for port and, when it arrived, Dona Luciana made for the beach with flowers and fruit and champagne and candles to give back to her mother, to complete the promise she would never, ever break again.

Twice a week the House of Father John is a place where Umbanda is practiced. For about an hour, the mediums dance and sing in a circle, while the drummers play the rhythms that salute and call each of the orixás in turn. As the drumming and the dancing and the singing heat up, caboclos that serve the orixás descend into the heads of the mediums, possessing their bodies, bringing the force, energy, and motion of the orixás. Now it is the entities, these caboclos representing the orixás, who dance; it is they whom the crowd watches and salutes, and it is they who depart when the drummers launch into the rhythms of farewell. And then the spirits of caboclos or old slaves or the exus and pomba-giras are called down to do their charitable work of advising, protecting, and healing. That is Umbanda, twice a week, at the House of Father John.

But several times a year the House of Father John celebrates Candomblé. On the Saturday night closest to the feast day of the saint associated with an orixá such as Omolu or Ogum, the House of Father John becomes the site of an all-night celebration. In the morning, the appropriate sacrifices and offerings are made. Food is cooked, the house decorated with paper streamers, fresh flowers, and green foliage; everything is made ready for the celebration of that orixá. The dancing starts late, around 11:00 p.m., but the benches are already mostly full by 10:00 p.m., as people filter in early in hopes of a good seat. As Seu Silva opens the festivities with a speech, praising the orixás, asking of them protection, prosperity, peace, and happiness, the air is electric. Seu Silva's homily is broken repeatedly by applause, then suddenly the drums break in, the dancing begins, and, as with the Umbanda session but with fantastically greater energy, caboclos representing the orixás descend and dance for three or four whirling, exhilarating, and exhausting hours. Finally, in the wee hours, the climax: One of the senior mediums, initiated some years earlier in the Candomblé, emerges from a little room where she has been in seclusion for a week. First she emerges as Oxalá, then twice more, as two different orixás, one of which will be the orixá to whom the celebration is devoted. For each, she is elaborately costumed, and all eyes are on her as she—or, rather, the orixá—dances and blesses all in the house. As the cocks crow and the sky first hints at dawn, the sacred foods associated with the orixás are served out on broad leaves, with ice cold beer to wash it down, to revive bodies and spirits drained by the night of celebration.

Dona Luciana does not celebrate the orixás with all-night rituals, nor does the House of Saint Benedict hold Candomblés on those Saturday nights around the feast days of Saint George or Santa Barbara. Dona Luciana respects Candomblé, but it, as she puts it, "is not my line. My line is lighter, more elevated." At the House of Saint Benedict, Candomblé is seen as African, primitive.

The orixás are honored at both those houses of White Umbanda, but their presence in ritual is much attenuated. As at the House of Father John, hymns are sung (but no drums are played) in turn for each of the orixás. At Dona Luciana's, caboclos representing the orixás do descend—but they do not dance. Ogum's servant, the Spanish crusader Hernán de la Arena, descends to spiritually secure the premises, followed by Oxossi's servant, the French priest who celebrates communion with all in attendance. The orixás themselves almost never appear;[8] according to Dona Luciana, their power, purity, and their radical difference from humankind makes them too dangerous, like fire or lava. At the House of Saint Benedict, the hymns are sung, some accompanied by soft clapping, but no caboclos descend to represent the orixás. There, it seems, the orixás, explicitly defined as vibrations, energies, forces of nature, have not only been divested of their identity as African deities but, as with all things that evoke Africa, pushed to the margins, silenced, washed white.

While the orixás in general are much less of a presence in White Umbanda, three of the orixás I listed above are completely absent from The House of Saint Benedict and Dona Luciana's, both of which are firmly in the line of White Umbanda. Their absence is striking, and indicative of fundamental differences of ideology and social context with Afro-Brazilian Umbanda.

One of the absent orixás is Oxumaré, the rainbow serpent. Granted, Oxumaré is not a central figure at the House of Father John—I never saw a medium possessed by Oxumaré—but there at least they maintain the assentamento for Oxumaré with great care, and there is a general familiarity with the deity. People know that Oxumaré carries water to the heavens, that Oxumaré is the rainbow, that he/she is conceived as a serpent devouring itself and/or rejuvenating itself periodically by shedding its skin, and that Oxumaré is male for six months, then female for six months, and therefore, according to several people who specifically elaborated on it, the patron and often the spiritual parent of gays, lesbians, and bisexuals.

What they know at the House of Father John about Oxumaré may explain his/her absence in White Umbanda. The history of White Umbanda has been one of systematically excluding those elements conflicting with respectable, middle-class morality and comportment. White Umbanda purged such practices as blood sacrifice, the ritual use of alcohol, loud drumming and dancing, while instituting modesty, charity, and a decidedly Roman Catholic morality. Middle-class propriety in all things, but especially in regard to sexuality and gender. Oxumaré—oscillating between the poles of male and female, not just ambiguous but explicitly bisexual—could never fit within such an ethos.

Oxumaré, I think, violates the implicit code of White Umbanda in other ways. White Umbanda prizes the high, the pure, and the evolved. Oxumaré is a serpent, and serpents are low, reptilian, eaters of dust, symbols of the phallus, of temptation, of danger. White Umbanda emphasizes the opposition of the spiritual and the material (and carnal) and equates the former with good, the latter with evil. What could be more material, more carnal, than the serpent? And what image could be more radically irrational and emblematic of the lustful hunger of life than the serpent devouring itself? Finally, reflecting its roots in Kardecite Spiritism and positivism, White Umbanda is infused with the ideology of order and progress, with time conceived as an arrow moving ever onward and upward. Oxumaré constructs time as a circle and life as an endless pattern of oscillation, male and female, death and rebirth; not progress, but renewal.

Ossaim, the orixá of medicinal and ritual plants, is also missing at Dona Luciana's and the House of Saint Benedict. There is some confusion as to Ossaim's gender. Cacciatore's *Diccionário* identifies Ossaim as masculine, as does Sangirardi's *Deuses da Africa no Brasil*. But as Sangirardi points out, the eminent Brazilian ethnographer Edison Carneiro identified Ossaim as feminine. Jim Wafer, in his study of Candomblé in Bahia, found that, at least among those he worked with, Ossaim, like Oxumaré, oscillates between male and female.[9] In his anthology of orixá mythology, Reginaldo Prandi consistently uses the masculine pronoun and adjective forms in referring to Ossaim.[10] That was true as well at the House of Father John, so, not having yet read Wafer, I assumed and still assume that there Ossaim is conceived of as male. If Ossaim were bisexual, I am sure someone would have brought it up.

Ossaim had one very important daughter at the House of Father John. That was Dona Linda, a woman in her late middle ages who was often referred to as Ossaim. I never witnessed Dona Linda possessed by Ossaim; in fact, I never saw her in trance at all. Ossaim manifested himself in Dona Linda in a thoroughly practical way, through a broad and detailed knowledge of medicinal and ritual plants, which Dona Linda collected in the nearby forests and mountains and valleys. She knew about lots and lots of different plants. She knew where to find them, when and how to harvest them (some, for example, must be picked on a waning moon, others are strongest during a full moon; some are picked in the morning, others in the afternoon, some anytime, and so forth), how to prepare them, what each is called, what each is good for, how best to use them. No doubt she acquired this knowledge through a lifetime of learning from others steeped in the centuries-old traditions of medicinal and ritual botany. But she traces her role as daughter of Ossaim, herbalist for the House of Father John, to a dramatic event that occurred some years back. Ossaim saved Dona Linda's life. Dona Linda, it seems, had suffered a bad cut on her leg and it became terribly infected. Living alone in a small shack, too feverish and delirious to leave and seek help, Dona Linda, knowing death was near, could do nothing but pray, until she passed into unconsciousness. When she came to, her fever and swelling much reduced, she noted that there were a number of medicinal plants in her shack. How they got there, she wasn't certain, but her belief was that at the height of her fever, when she was too delirious to remember, Ossaim had given her the strength and knowledge to go out and gather the plants she needed to heal herself.

The efficacy of Dona Linda's medicinal plants and the power of Ossaim are renowned at the House of Father John, and yet the healing powers of this orixá go unmentioned in White Umbanda. Why? In part the answer may lie in social history. For Dona Linda, and for many if not most of the participants at the House of Father John, knowledge of and reliance on herbal remedies is nothing new or esoteric; they grew up with it, just as their parents and grandparents did in the rural areas from which many of them came. It is part of Afro-Brazilian culture, and rural culture generally. But for the thoroughly urban, mostly middle-class white folks at Dona Luciana's and the House of Saint Benedict, herbs are for cooking. For them, plants are not powerful; they are either pretty or tasty and, if neither, then of no consequence at all.

In part, though, the absence of Ossaim points to ideology, at two levels. First, the same positivist, "scientific" current that runs so deeply in White Umbanda places high value and invests deep faith in Western medicine. While the spirits deal with the spiritual aspects of illness, doctors and pharmaceuticals are entrusted with the biological dimension of disease. (For example, a few weeks after I first began working with Dona Luciana, I developed a sore throat, probably from the diesel fumes and exhaust from all the cars and buses cramped in the concrete canyons of Copacabana. I mentioned this to Dona Luciana—"Ah!" she said, "We can take care of that." She went into her bedroom, where the altar was; I expected her to do something spiritual, I was curious as to what it would be. She came out moments later with a drawer full of medicines and picked out some pills and lozenges. On another occasion she sent me to see her own doctor and, on another, to an ear/nose/throat specialist she knew.) For true believers in doctors and drugs and procedures, Ossaim's plants are folklore, old wifery, "home remedies" at best and worthless or dangerous at worst.

The other, related, ideological dimension, of course, involves the kind of stigmatization of Afro-Brazilian traditions we discussed earlier, exemplified by Macedo's shocked testimony,[11] and the old slave Mané's comments about purifying Umbanda of its African elements. Ossaim, and the herbal lore he/she represents, are deeply African in fact and in imagination. No wonder Ossaim is absent from White Umbanda.

Finally, the orixá Tempo is absent from White Umbanda.

Tempo is the Portuguese word for time. It also means weather. Tempo is embodied in a great old tree out back of the House of Father John. I was first introduced to Tempo one night by Elena, a young medium (she had just turned twenty at the time) who receives a caboclo spirit known as the *Boiadeiro do Tempo*, The Cowboy of Time. I was talking to Boiadeiro one night; he gave me some encouraging advice, and told me to go light a candle at Tempo, out back. People were often told to do this, so I asked Boiadeiro what Tempo was all about. He put his hand on my neck, drew his face close to mine, blew a big cloud of cigar smoke at me, and told me to ask his horse (medium) after he left her that night. So I did. Elena took me out to the big tree. "Tempo runs through everything past, present, and future," she said. "See how Tempo's roots go down into the earth? Well they go all the way down and under this mountain and under the oceans and all the way to Angola, to Angola now, and to Angola when our ancestors lived there before they were brought here, and back to the beginning of everything. Look up the trunk." I looked up the enormous trunk, up and up. "See how the branches reach out to the sky? They stretch invisibly to all the stars. The stars are Tempo's leaves. The branches reach into space and time, to the future, infinite."

Elena's comments might give the impression that Tempo is serene, calm, like an infinite sea of time and space. No beginning, no end, no boundaries; the troubles of a life are but a tick of Tempo's clock. Peace.

But I would come to learn that my initial impression was incorrect or, rather, radically incomplete.

Only once did I see Tempo incorporate at the House of Father John. It was very late, after midnight, and only a handful of us were present. We were out at Tempo's tree, where Seu Silva would sacrifice a rooster to Tempo. Fernando cradled the drum between his knees as he played. After cutting the bird's throat and letting its blood splatter over the big altar at the base of the tree, Seu Silva handed the fowl over to Orlando, who cut off its wings and feet (the organs of locomotion) and head (the seat of consciousness), cut out its liver (the source of blood, in folk belief), and the heart that beats life, arranging the parts on a little iron brazier (a reminder of the grill on which Saint Lawrence was roasted) in a clay bowl, which he placed on the altar. It was a starkly beautiful arrangement, the head and the wings suggesting a living bird, the little grill where its body would have been emphatically representing the iron truth of death. And it was a strange and awesome moment. A shiver ran down my spine and I felt a cold heavy dread (like in one of those dreams where you dream you are sleeping and something ominous is in the room and you try to move but you can't, and you feel whatever dangerous thing it is coming closer and closer) and then there was a deep, deep, anguished moan. In the dream you make an ungodly groan, and it frees your muscles; but, in this moment, the groan came from several feet away. I looked over; in the candlelight, Seu Silva bent over and straightened up, bent over again, like a tree bending to the breaking point in the wind. He straightened and bent and started a slow, heavy dance, his feet rooted, and then one foot would uproot, he would almost fall over, like a drunk about to pitch over onto the ground. I looked at his face. His skin was flushed and leathery, his eyes glassy. He looked bewildered, in agony, insane, drunk, and terribly strong. I was frightened, appalled, and full of helpless compassion for his suffering. It was Tempo.

The word I most often heard associated with Tempo at the House of Father John was *verdade* (truth). Tempo, it seems, tells hard truths about existence, truths that are inescapable (after all, if Tempo is beginning and end, earth and cosmos, then his truth is *the* truth of how it is). His dance, with its breaking and bending, represents what the weather of this world does to us—sometimes the weather is fair and kind, but at times it blows us around, bends us double, uproots us, and, a few times in most of our lives, it breaks us. And one last time breaks us forever. Rarely do we see Tempo—I saw him only that one time—and, like the nightmare we dismiss as just a bad dream and forget about until next time, we forget Tempo until we come face to face at some dreadful moment. Tempo is the god that drinks, and he is not a gentle drunk. As weather, he rages—in the hurricane that drowns a city, in the drought that starves a country, in the earthquake that kills ten thousand. And Tempo goes on forever, but at some point he leaves each of us sprawled in the dirt. Tempo is truth.

White Umbanda sees truth in order, rationality, progress, propriety, charity, and optimism. Tempo suggests that the world, the cosmos, as well as we ourselves, are quite otherwise. As Jim Wafer points out, Tempo is a homeless god, "abject," living in the street.[12] Like that homeless, crazed, bearded man who stomped and cursed and glared up at me on my balcony, Tempo, it seems, holds up a mirror that White Umbanda would rather not look into.

Ogum is your father, Oxum is your mother: that is what they told me. Dona Luciana, Seu Silva, the spirits Jurema, Mané, Golden Mountain, Gerônimo; they all said the same thing. Ogum, with Oxum. As an anthropologist employing the participant observation methodology, I include under "participation" not only taking part in rituals, but also making the concepts and thought-ways of Umbanda part of my thinking and perception, and observing their effects.[13] So I took seriously these statements that Ogum is my father, Oxum my mother, and, like the Umbandistas I knew, I used those notions to think about and know myself.

It was easy for me to see Oxum in myself. Oxum is vain, drawn to luxury and sensual pleasure. She is also nurturing, agreeable, kind, and graceful. Oxum seeks comfort, tranquility, harmony; she creates a space around her, a domestic space where these qualities flourish.

Ogum I could not see, or did not want to see. Ogum is a warrior, and as such he is violent, hot tempered, he acts too often out of passion, not reason. His passion sometimes blinds him, makes him stupid and cruel. One myth tells how Ogum returned to his city after a long campaign, expecting the joyous welcome due a victorious warrior. He was greeted with silence. No feast, no women—not even a word. Enraged, he drew his sword and lay about, till the streets ran with blood and almost no one was left alive. When the sun set, a committee of survivors approached him, pleading with him to stop. It seems he had forgotten that on this day of the year, the people were sworn by the gods to maintain complete silence. Stupid, bloody bastard. Devastated by guilt, he thrust his bloody sword into the ground and disappeared through that wound in the ground to land in the sky, an orixá.[14]

Ogum has good qualities as well; he has guts, he endures, he possesses boundless energy and optimism. Ogum is resourceful and down to earth. Ogum wins the battle. But he does not always reap the rewards. He is unlucky in love—remember the story about the nine Iansás and the seven Ogums? There are many, many more, where Ogum loses out to his rival Xangô. Ogum is too straightforward, too simple, so he loses out in politics as well. One myth tells of the very old days, when humans and orixás lived together on earth. These were good times, so the population grew and grew. But that meant new lands would have to be cleared, and people and gods only had tools of copper and stone, and the going was tough. Ogum, though, knew the secret of iron. His axes and plows saved the day, and he shared his secret; from that day forward, all would be fed, and fed plenty. The orixás made him king of the orixás and humankind. A king is regal, well dressed, politic, smooth—like his rival Xangô. But Ogum was a simple man. He loved to hunt. He went out one morning and came back days later, dirty, ragged, bloody, tired, and happy. The orixás, those fine folk, were aghast. Maybe he had saved gods and humankind, but a dirty, sweaty, ragged king? No way. Ogum was dethroned.

I resisted this consensus that Ogum was my father and that I am in deep ways made in his image. Resistance, the psychoanalysts tell us, is often a sign that one is approaching uncomfortable and important truth. But surely I am not like Ogum, bloody warrior, sweaty farmer, all force and fight? I pride myself on being rational, in control of my emotions, not violent, an intellectual (a professor!), subtle—and on and on. But as I lived with this Umbanda idea, Ogum is your father, more and more he pushed his way through the cracks in my self image, pushing me a little closer to honesty about myself. Not violent? Not now, but as a child, my fists were busy. Certainly my emotions have often driven me to do stupid things, hurtful things for which I am forever guilty. Subtle, sophisticated, an intellectual? I read a lot, I think a lot, but among my peers, I feel clumsy, an unkempt, sweaty Ogum, out of place among those polished, natural orixás of the academy. And, yes, I could match Ogum tale for tale on the subject of bad luck in love.

As I continued to participate in this Umbanda way of thinking, these truths about myself, my foibles, came gradually (it took a lot of time, and the process continues) to bother me less and less, in much the same way that the stuttering that crippled me for many years is now just an oddity, laughable. At the same time, I came more and more to recognize those other Ogum traits—optimism, passion, guts, energy, persistence—that have seen me through so much. Yes, Dona Luciana, Jurema, Gerônimo, Mané—Ogum is my father, Oxum my mother.

Blood and Water

quanto sangue derramado	how much blood has spilled
em cima deste frio chão?	on this cold ground?
onde mora Tranca Rua,	where does Tranca Rua live
o meu patrão?	my patron?
mora lá no portão	he lives there, at the front gate.

It was quiet and cool and just about midnight when I heard Seu Silva singing about blood and Tranca Rua, his rough voice wafting in from the gate outside the House of Father John. The forty or so people who had come to consult the spirits that night had left, as had most of the mediums. Only a handful of the most senior mediums—along with Jorge, Fernando the drummer, and me—were left still inside, barefoot on the packed dirt floor of the *barracão* (the main ritual space), as the soft night breeze lifted Seu Silva's hymn to Tranca Rua. We followed the sound out to the gate. There on a low stool, his sanguine complexion even redder in the candlelight, sat Seu Silva, a large clay bowl of manioc flour stained reddish orange from *azeite de dendê* (red palm oil) at the feet of his thick short legs. Fernando handed Seu Silva a young live chicken. Seu Silva took a swig from his beer, wiped his mouth on his sleeve, and picked up a sturdy knife. Holding the chicken above the bowl, he cut its throat, letting the blood spurt over the offering, and then on the gate, and, finally, with the last drops he sprinkled the street that runs by the gate in front of the House of Father John.

FLUIDIFIED WATER

It was quiet and cool and nearly nine o'clock as we sat in our pews in the bluish half light at the House of Saint Benedict, as each of the four mediums in turn approached Dona Lisa and touched their foreheads to the gleaming linoleum at her feet, before rising to a knee to kiss her hand and receive her blessing. Behind her loomed a larger-than-life statue of Christ, arms reaching out toward us, palms open in a gesture of peace and benediction, dressed in flowing ivory robes, crowned with a glass halo of blue gaslight and framed with great vases of fresh flowers. As the last medium took her leave of their elderly mother, plump, bald, Seu Gomes emerged from the altar room. Well-versed in Cabalistic and other esoteric lore, avid reader of European history, and enthusiastic fan and player of old-time jazz, and, as always on session nights, redolent of lavender and rosewater, Seu Gomes padded out in his white cotton slippers, a heavy, blue-tinged glass carafe in his hand. To each of us he offered a sip of *agua fluidificada* (fluidified water), remarking on the lightness it imparts to spirit and body.

BLOOD AND WATER

A river of blood divides White Umbanda from Afro-Brazilian Umbanda. At the House of Father John, the relationship between persons and the orixás is mediated at the most crucial junctures through animal sacrifice. Blood is life, and not only metaphorically. When it is spilled, life and death meet, and with them come together the cosmic and the mundane, the sacred and profane, human being and orixá. In that moment before death extinguishes the life-force, a burst of spiritual energy spurts forth, revitalizing the living connection with the spiritual world.

That is nothing but error, a misguided and unnecessary practice, according to the adepts of White Umbanda at the House of Saint Benedict. They voice their objection in three registers. One, a voice of rational argument, asks what purely spiritual beings, the orixás, could possibly gain from these sacrifices. Blood has force, but it is biological force, material;

the orixá force is cosmic, nonmaterial, spiritual. Those who practice sacrifice are doing nothing but killing, and, indeed, doing worse than nothing but killing: these practices attract the lowest kinds of spiritual entities, earn bad karma, and envelop the practitioner with the negative spiritual energies surrounding death. Another register voices aesthetic objections: sacrifice is *pesado* (heavy), and grim and dirty—precisely the opposite of the White Umbanda taste for the *leve* (light), the happy, the clean. Blood sacrifice is, to White Umbanda, viscerally repugnant. A third register frames the objection in moralistic, judgmental terms, often tinged with racial biases: sacrifice is "cruel," "ignorant," "superstitious," part of the sorcerer's arsenal at worst, at best just wrong. It is "barbaric," and, whether explicitly stated or not, it goes without saying that it is a relic of Africa practiced by Afro-Brazilians. Spilling blood? Not in the true Umbanda, Seu Gomes concludes: "pure water from a spring, waters in which rose petals have steeped, waters with drops of perfume—those are the fluids pleasing to the evolved entities that we work with. Blood? My entities would not come near it!"

The opposition of blood and water crystallizes a broader opposition between White Umbanda and Afro-Brazilian Umbanda practices for mediating the mundane and the spiritual. Afro-Brazilian Umbanda connects with the spiritual through the organic symbolism of blood, plants, food, and the voluptuous envelopment and mobilization of the body and its senses. White Umbanda opts for the "light" and "clean"; the subtle hint of perfume, the purity of water, the body stilled. Water, not blood. What can this opposition mean?

EXU

Tranca Rua, the "patron" who lives at the front gate about whom Seu Silva was singing, is an exu. Exu is a trickster, the intermediary between human beings and orixás, and represents the principle of movement, vitality, expansion, and growth. Exu is needy, horny, amoral, tragic, funny, and contradictory. The Russian folklorist Michael Bakhtin, I think, would see in exu, or at least some exus, an emblem of the carnivalesque that inverts and ridicules the status quo, and an emblem of the grotesque body, all appetites and passion.[1] Freud no doubt would read exu as id, and would thus concur with the ubiquitous Umbanda refrain: *sem Exu, não se faz nada* (without Exu, nothing is done).

So before any serious work in Umbanda—before a session, before making an offering—homage is paid to Exu. Dona Lisa, an adept of White Umbanda, lights a black and red candle and offers Exu a cigar and a shot of cachaça in a little cranny by the gate. The offering is meant to facilitate the evening's work, but also to placate Exu, to keep him from interfering, from letting loose with his trickster antics. I think Dona Lisa finds Exu's appetite for cigars and liquor distasteful, morally unfortunate; as she puts it, although her exu is "elevated," he still has material yearnings that must be satisfied, because, without Exu, nothing is done.

That's White Umbanda. Seu Silva's Tranca Rua has rather a lustier appetite. The offering, or *despacho*, that precedes any event where something is done, minimally involves the bowl of manioc flour with palm oil and onions, the blood of the sacrificed chicken, a cigar, and usually a bottle—or at least a glass—of cachaça. The manioc flour accompanies almost any Brazilian meal, but it is a bedrock staple of the peasant and the poor, while red palm oil is the emblematic ingredient of Afro-Brazilian cuisine—it is, in fact, a metonym for Bahia, the heart of Candomblé in the popular imagination. Onions are pungent, strong, from under the ground; and the chicken's blood represents the force of life and spirit. Cachaça and cigars represent earthly indulgences, lively vices. Tranca Rua's meal, then, is redolent of Afro-Brazil, of strong appetites and pungent satisfaction, bohemian pleasures, and the force of life and transformation.

Most nights, midnight marks the end of the work at the House of Father John, and, indeed, the regular session had been over for more than an hour on that night when Seu Silva sang and sacrificed for Tranca Rua. But this Monday midnight marked the beginning of very serious work. This was the week of Tranca Rua, the exu-in-chief of the House of Father

John. Held every year in May, it is at once a community celebration of this powerful protector and facilitator and a reaffirmation of the individual relationships between each medium and their personal exus. Finally, fundamentally, it is a recharging, a rebirth, through blood and death, of the spiritual life of the House of Father John, mediated through the communion of Tranca Rua and Seu Silva. It is, also, a week in which the organic symbolism so characteristic of Afro-Brazilian Umbanda becomes overwhelmingly salient. Before returning to our discussion of that week, I want contrast the sensual, embodied dimensions of ritual practice in Afro-Brazilian and White Umbanda.

THE HOUSE OF FATHER JOHN

There is a striking contrast between Afro-Brazilian and White Umbanda's stances toward the body, toward the relationship between the sensual, the material, and the spiritual, as reflected not so much in explicit statements, but much more through the aesthetics of ritual. Afro-Brazilian Umbanda embraces, energizes, engulfs the body, enveloping it in a stew of sensations; White Umbanda quiets the body, minimizes it, subordinates it in a Cartesian dualism of mind and body, in which the mind—equated with spirit—is the good, and is good to the degree that it is free of the body's gross materiality. Oftentimes, listening to Ronaldo or Seu Gomes elaborating on the levels and lines and planes that structure the spiritual in their minds, I felt as though they would happily erase their bodies and inscribe instead the geometry of a bloodless cosmos. But in Afro-Brazilian Umbanda, which also categorically opposes the material and the spiritual, the spiritual is always mediated through the material, and especially through the body, through its movements, its senses, and through its living presence in spiritual space.

It is after eight as I pass the gate at the House of Father John. The night is warm, though it is the middle of winter, or what passes for winter in Rio. Just inside is a little house for exu, a few feet high and wide and deep, the front open but enclosed by iron bars. A statue of Tranca Rua and a statue of pomba-gira are inside; between them, at their feet, are a burning cigar, a shot of cachaça, a clay bowl filled with an offering of manioc flour, onions, azeite de dendê, and the wings, head, feet, heart, liver, and blood of a white chicken. Wafting from the cage, the odors are strong, complex, and pleasant.

I make my way inside, into the barracão, the main room, its architecture evocative of a number of symbolically loaded spaces. The packed dirt floor refers to the clearings in the woods, the terreiros, where slaves surreptitiously (or not) held both sacred and profane dances remembered from Africa. It refers also to the cleared spaces of Indian villages; when the Indian spirits are celebrated, the dirt floor is blanketed with leaves and the space referred to as *aldeia* (village). And it refers to the dirt floor of the senzala, the slave quarters, the place where the ancestors passed their hours when not laboring in the fields and mines. One walks barefoot on the dirt during rituals, earth and flesh energetically connected. During torrential rains, enough water leaks through the roof to leave mud puddles and fill the air with the dank smell of wet clay. But tonight it's dry; instead of that thick flinty smell of clay, my nose is stung for a moment as I walk past the hide of a goat, stretched on the wall, sacrificed a few weeks earlier. The reek fades into the background in a few minutes, as the odors of coffee, offerings of flowers and food in various states of freshness and decay, burnt wax from the ubiquitous candles, the distinctive tobacco aromas of the old slaves' pipes and the Indians' cigars, laid down like sediments, session after session, and the odors of the people with me—the perfumes, soaps, their breath and perspiration, the subtle and unique airs that come off living beings—envelop the moment. It is like a *moqueca*, the classic Afro-Brazilian dish that combines green peppers and very hot peppers, tomatoes, onions, garlic, ginger, fish and shellfish, coconut milk, and, of course, azeite de dendê—strong, complex, a harmony that leaves all its notes distinct but subtly blended, compelling, alive. Embraces and smiles, deep looks and soft conversations flow with the smells until the session starts.

Starts with a yell and a bang and a smell: song, smoke, and drums. The voice of Fernando, the drummer, breaks above the murmur with a call to Ogum to fumigate his children with the smoke of the aromatic herbs *arruda* and *guiné*.[2] As Fernando's tenor soars, he and his two colleagues attack their drums, and a rolling, clopping beat, a sonic mirror of Ogum's mythical warrior persona, fills the air and then the muscles, nerves, and viscera. Mariana, a senior medium and figure of considerable force and dignity, makes her way through the barracão with a big censor fashioned from a two-liter can, filled with charcoal and streaming great clouds of incense, arruda, guiné, and other herbs. Mariana works her way through the crowd, thoroughly fumigating each and every person.

The drums break into a series of *toques*, or rhythms, for each of the orixás in succession as the mediums dance in a circle on the dirt floor of the terreiro. Their dances pantomime myth; their movements are large, powerful, energetic, physical. Sweat pours and hearts pound. A medium might fall into trance as the toque for her orixá is played; her dance becomes total, her body the unrestrained vehicle of spirit. These moments, lasting up to several minutes, are electrifying, the focus of all eyes, and they are exhausting; when the orixá leaves the medium, she is often left limp, soaked in sweat, spent. All the while, the drums and the dancers and the audience—they sing along, and clap, and sometimes members will break into convulsive trance as well—create a densely layered field for sensual, bodily immersion.

THE HOUSE OF SAINT BENEDICT

It is pin-drop quiet as we sit in the polished wood pews before the weekly session at the House of Saint Benedict. In front of us a low wooden railing separates the audience—which is very small, rarely more than a handful or so—from the open floor where the hymns and dances are performed and where people consult with the old slaves and Indians. But unlike the House of Father John, the floor here is not dirt; it is immaculately scrubbed and waxed linoleum, clean enough to eat off of. It fairly gleams in the still semidarkness, discretely illuminated by soft spotlights aimed at the larger than life figure of Christ, a bluish gas tube halo above his head, vases of lilies and roses and gladiolus at his feet. Barely audible at first, hidden speakers whisper forth a flowing arrangement of strings and flute. Seu Gomes glides out of a room off to the side, dressed all in white, cotton slippers on his feet. He approaches the rail, a beatific half smile and soft twinkle in his eye. With a slow graceful sweep of his hand, he summons us to the railing and, dipping into a silver chalice, sprinkles us each with drops of lavender water. It is the first, small smell—just a whiff of fragrance—and the only one I detect until the Indian spirits light their cigars an hour later. We take our seats, the mediums enter, and before long they are singing hymns to each orixás in turn. There are no drums; hand clapping accompanies a few of the hymns. Most are slow, sung in minor key, mournful to my ear. The dances are done in place with stiff, shuffling little steps. No one goes into trance during this ritual; no caboclos descend to perform the dances of the orixás. It is as though bodies and voices are barely there, mere traces of materiality set against the ethereal spiritual vision of the House of Saint Benedict. I watch from afar, connecting with the disembodied scene by the slenderest sensory thread and the distanced voice of abstract thought.

WAYS AND MEANS, BODY AND SPIRIT

Umbanda discourse makes a categorical and morally laden distinction between the material and the spiritual. That is as true at the Afro-Brazilian House of Father John as it is for the White Umbanda of the House of Saint Benedict. The body is just a vehicle; what matters is the spirit that animates it, coexists with it, survives its death, returns through reincarnations, and seeks ever higher levels of evolution and purity. Seu Silva repeatedly reminds the audience that we—our bodies, our breathing, feeling lives—will be dust on the road one day. What counts is spirit. Sometimes he sounds like Saint Augustine, or some ascetic monk, renouncing the body for the glory of the soul. And, indeed, Umbanda, whether Afro-Brazilian or White, does not celebrate the body, does not exalt its pleasures, does not make it equal partners with mind or spirit; neither, certainly, does it challenge the Western dichotomy of matter and spirit—it underlines it. But there is a difference. If at the House of Saint Benedict, the body is minimalized, its sensuality and sensual inputs restricted and narrowly channeled, almost to the vanishing point as though its diminishment would bring a corresponding increase of spirit, at the House of Father John the body is exuberantly present, because it is through the body that spirituality is accessed, channeled, made available to living people.

Let's examine some examples of the widely differing degrees and manners in which the two Umbandas mobilize the body in the interest of spirit:

Passes

Drawing from spiritualist metaphysics, many Umbandistas visualize the person as composed of a material body (flesh, blood, and organs), a spirit, and a *perispirit* (a kind of colorless membrane enveloping the body and mediating between it and the spirit). Disturbances in the body or the spirit, whether from disease, bad habits, negative thinking, ill will and envy directed toward the self from others, injurious attacks from negative spirits, trauma, or the mundane stresses and moral ambiguities of daily life, contaminate the perispirit. This sounds bad, and it is, but it is also fortunate, because the perispirit can be cleaned and brought into balance by Umbanda spirits through a routine operation called a passe.

Ronaldo's spirits give exemplary White Umbanda passes. Seven Arrows, for example, begins by placing one hand ever so close to your forehead, but not touching. His hand trembles, almost buzzes, from the energy of its contact with the perispirit. He then runs both hands down your chest—again, not touching, but buzz-trembling—then takes your fingers and pulls down sharply and firmly, the jolt going up your arms and into your shoulders. He turns you around and from behind begins a rhythmic finger snapping, slow, his hands moving in a rolling, smoothing, motion that your ears track by way of the snapping and that your body tracks by that uncanny feeling of presence without actual contact, like the sensation of passing under a low limb that nearly touches the top of your head but doesn't, raising a little shiver in the back of your neck. He continues, snapping from head to toe, occasionally picking away at some bad stuff visible only to spirits, and then finishes with another sharp tug on your fingers and a firm hug. The tugs are the only bodily contact. Seven Feathers is a little unusual in that practically all Indian spirits blow cigar smoke over the patient as part of the passe, while he abstains from tobacco. His artistry at evoking a kind of quasi-tactile imagination is exquisite; but the major outlines of his passe—the passing of the hands up and down the surface of the body, without touching or (quite commonly) touching only very lightly in a way that emphasizes not the surface of the skin but the perispirit that is visualized as enveloping the body, treating front and back, and tugging on the fingers—are standard in White Umbanda, in keeping with its aesthetics of "lightness" and its suppression of the body.

Passes at the Afro-Brazilian House of Father John are palpably "heavier," much more physical. Vivaldo's Indian spirit, Seven Arrows, briskly whisks away at the perispirit's impurities with palm fronds and leafy branches. To finish her passes, Joana's Cowgirl of Time envelops her head and mine in her long hair as though it were a hood, grasps my head around the ears and cheek, presses her forehead to mine, and shakes until I feel it all the way to my knees. Mariana's caboclo, Anaconda, throws her arms around me and squeezes like a vise—like an anaconda—as she lifts me off my feet. At the House of Father John, spirits are cleansed and restored through the warm, strong, embracing, enveloping connecting of bodies.

Banhos (baths)

In the evening, pluck the petals of a fresh yellow rose, one that hasn't started to fade, into a bowl of water. Place the bowl on your altar and light a candle. In the morning, take a regular shower

and then pour the rose water over you. You can do the same with
a white rose; the yellow rose carries the energies of Oxum (orixá
of fertility and fresh water); the white rose, the forces of Oxalá.
(Dona Luciana; White Umbanda)

Or:

Fill a clean, white, ceramic bowl with water. Add seven pieces of
rock salt, pure, without iodine, or seven drops of lavender. Let it
rest overnight and, in the morning, bathe your head in the water
. . . another good one is simply pure water from a waterfall—full
of the energies of Mama Oxum. Or just bathe in the waterfall,
letting Oxum wash over you. (Seu Gomes, White Umbanda)

Banhos are an ubiquitous part of Umbanda spiritual hygiene, cleansing, fortifying, bringing watery essences and energies to bear on the inner
and the spiritual by way of the surfaces of the body. Often they are liquid
metonyms of spiritual forces, a part evoking the whole, as, for example,
the water from the cascade connecting the bather to Oxum, orixá of fertility, fresh water, luxury, sweetness. Banhos are personal rituals, performed
in private, quite often at the very beginning of the day.

Dona Luciana and Seu Gomes both emphasize that the banhos they
prescribe are light, clean, refreshing, simple. Baths such as those described
are also prescribed at the House of Father John, but there are others, pungent, organic, "heavy" in Seu Gomes's disapproving characterization:

Go to the weekly street market. Talk to one of those ladies who
sells the herbs down at the end of the stalls. Buy a bunch of basil.
Take the bunch home. Sit on the floor in front of your altar and
light a candle. Place the basil in a big clay bowl of water and
calmly work it and shred until it's just little bits and green liquid.
In the morning, shower and then pour it over your head. (Zé,
Afro-Brazilian Umbanda)

That would strengthen your mental powers, Zé assured me, good for when writing and researching and thinking leave you dull and tired. When I went to buy the basil, the herb vendor asked: "to cook with, or for a banho?"

To sweeten love, steep honey in water for three days. On the third night, add red rose petals. In the morning, take a shower and then bathe with the honeyed rose water, being sure to bath the whole body, understand? *Every part*, you see? (Elena, Afro-Brazilian Umbanda)

One night I go to the House of Father John a little early. Zé is sitting with a man whose face is swollen. His lip is split and his mouth droops open on one side. Zé gently sponges a green liquid from a bowl onto the man's face as he softly prays. The green liquid is an infusion of medicinal herbs collected by Dona Linda, a daughter of Ossaim, orixá of the plants used in healing and ritual. These infusions, called *amacis*, can steep for days, even weeks, becoming pungent, potent, even slimy and putrid.

The honey and rose petal baths, such as those described by Dona Luciana and Seu Gomes, are largely symbolic—metaphoric and metonymic connections of honey with sweetness, red roses with sexuality, as suggested by the injunction to bathe *every part*, Elena being too modest to be more specific when talking to me, a male acquaintance. The basil and the green liquid, however, are steeped in Afro-Brazilian traditions of herbal medicine, which White Umbanda largely eschews; indeed, Seu Gomes dismissed Zé's basil bath as not only "heavy," but "silly" and coming from "people lacking in science."

Sacudimento (shaking)

There is another procedure common in Afro-Brazilian Umbanda that works the spiritual through the application of materials to the surface of the skin. Sacudimentos are complex rituals, composed of offerings, prayers, songs—and symbolically loaded materials. They are meant to dis-charge negative energy, to cleanse, to heal, to strengthen, like a banho, but these are much more elaborate rituals, and they are not private matters performed in one's shower. If banhos pour a cleansing bowl of metaphor and metonym over the surface of the body, sacudimentos flood the person in swirling currents of symbolic reference.

For example, on a late afternoon I wander out back of the House of Father John. Dona Linda, the child of Ossaim, the orixá of medicinal and ritual plants, is arranging the materials for a sacudimento that will be performed later that evening. There is a lot of stuff—various bowls of different colored beans, rice, an herbal infusion like the one Zé applied to that man's swollen face, candles—all kinds of things:

- Black-eyed peas for Oxum, orixá of fresh flowing water and fertility.

- Red beans and purple beans for Nanã, the Grandmother orixá who lives in the still waters and the mud, bringer of wealth and mature serenity.

- Little brown beans (called *mulatinhos*, little mulattos) for the warrior Ogum; white ones for the sky god Oxalá, black ones for the old slave who will preside over the ritual.

Each type of offering is in its own clay bowl: a bowl of white rice, for Oxalá; a large clay bowl, almost two feet in diameter, filled with cut cab-bage, beets, turnips, yams, manioc tubers, and various other roots for the Indian spirits (the vegetables represent the products of their forest gardens); another large clay bowl for the old slaves containing sugar and coffee—the cash crops of the plantation economy—and manioc flour, the starchy staple whose empty calories sustained the slaves.

There are twenty-one white candles, white representing purity, and Oxalá; twenty-one because that is the product of the mystical numbers

3 and 7. There are seven red candles and seven black candles for exu, the trickster who mediates between humans and orixás, without whom nothing is done. There are also seven onions, quartered, for exu.

An enamel basin contains an infusion of *fortuna* and *mamona* leaves. Fortuna, as the name implies, brings good fortune; the foods for the orixás are often served on broad mamona leaves.

In addition to all these items, there are seven raw eggs, in the shell (eggs absorb bad energies like sponges), seven pieces of pemba, a chalk imported from Africa, a live rooster and a live hen, and a gunpowder crayon.

A man—not one of the regulars at the House of Father John at the time—is led out to the back, where we are, by a couple of mediums. He is barefoot, dressed in old clothes. He looks to be in the younger part of middle age, but tired, his eyes dull and sad. In his posture, the heaviness of his movements, his face, I read a long stretch of loss, worry, despair, guilt, and self-reproach. But I don't know his case, the specifics of his troubles; I just know he looks battered by life, a man who has been drinking from the bottom of its barrel. They have him stand in the middle of a cleared square of hard-packed dirt, and place a torchlike affair with a thick candle at its end in his hand and light it. Orlando, one of the mediums, carefully draws gunpowder designs—a six-pointed star, crossed arrows, a bow, some wavy lines representing water, the double-edged hatchet of Xangô, in a circle around the man, connecting each design with a thin trace of gunpowder. Orlando checks his work and goes inside, while Dona Linda and a couple of other women arrange the candles in lines and blocks outside the circle. They light the candles and leave the man, standing, holding his candle torch.

Time passes—the late afternoon is gone, it's dark—and Orlando returns with Fernando the drummer and several mediums. Orlando is in trance; it is José Mineiro, an old slave and sorcerer, who uses Orlando's body. José takes a seat on a low three-legged stool, downs a swig of red wine from a little black bowl, and starts singing in low, slurry tones, as though drunk or addled with age or both: "*José Mineiro, velho feiticeiro*"

(José mineiro, old sorcerer). Over and over. They bring him the hen; José Mineiro slits its throat, drizzles its blood on the slab, and arranges its head, feet, wings, and heart in a bowl for exu. He does the same with the rooster, all the while singing his little verse. They take the bowls to the gate; José takes another drink of wine and mutters—the time's come. Fernando's drum beats out, and he sings: "*Descarrega descarrega meu Santo Antonio*" (Discharge, discharge [that is, take away the bad energy] my Saint Anthony). As the chorus is taken up, the amaci is dumped over the man; the water runs down his face, down his back, green vegetation sticking in his hair. Each of the bowls of beans is spilled over his head; the eggs are broken over him; the bowl of cabbages, turnips, beets, and yams, and the bowl of sugar, coffee, and manioc all follow. One of the mediums takes a knife and rips the man's shirt, his pants, the others tearing at the rent fabric, Fernando's drum swelling and speeding up with the chorus, it's all a swirl of stuff and sound and then the gunpowder goes off and everyone shakes their clothes and a few of the mediums break into the cackling, belly laughs of exu and pomba-gira, and then—it stops. The man is led inside, dripping, stuff clinging to his clothes and skin and dropping to the ground. He washes and dresses in clean new clothes. Everything is swept up and disposed of in the bushes, along with the man's old clothes. He comes back outside some time later, quiet, drained, but looking much relieved. He even smiles. He chats with Seu Silva and shakes Orlando's hand; he then walks out into the night, clean, combed, well dressed, with no visible indication of the messy ritual he had undergone or the troubles that brought him to it.

At one level the passes, banhos, and sacudimentos in White Umbanda and Afro-Brazilian Umbanda are of a piece. In both styles, the spiritual is mediated through the material, through various substances in contact with the body. The substances and the ritual practices constitute a code of metaphors and metonyms, fluently deployed, interpretable at multiple levels, ranging from the particular—the honey and rose petals to quicken passion, implying passion's absence—to the general metaphysic of spirit, perispirit, and body traced by Ronaldo's hands as he gives a passe. But at the level of style, Afro-Brazilian Umbanda and White Umbanda stand in stark contrast. In the former we can read an immersion in the senses, an embracing of the body, and an elaboration of material signifiers; in the latter, a withdrawal, a minimalization, an abstract and disembodied code.

"GIVE BLOOD TO EXU"

The relationship between an Umbanda medium and her or his exu (or its female counterpart, pomba-gira) is close. Personal, and crucial. This is as true in White Umbanda as it is in Afro-Brazilian Umbanda—after all, without Exu, nothing is done. Dona Luciana is most solicitous of Mari-Carmen, the *flamenca* dancer pomba-gira that she receives once a month. Dona Luciana's gifts to Mari-Carmen include real Spanish castanets, a flamenca dancer's costume, jewelry, dancing shoes, perfume, all kinds of things. When Mari-Carmen incorporates in Dona Luciana, Ronaldo presents her with seven long-stemmed yellow roses, politely pointing out that they are a gift from Dona Luciana. In Dona Luciana's White Umbanda, the reciprocal relationship of medium and pomba-gira or exu is mediated through gifts, through the medium serving as a vehicle for the spirit, through the spirit offering protection and efficacy.

That is all also true at the Afro-Brazilian House of Father John, but spirit and medium are further bonded through body and blood. That bond is renewed, reenergized, every year during the week of Tranca Rua through a ritual performed individually by each and every medium. The ritual is referred to simply as "confirming" the exu and pomba-gira. The words of one of the songs that is used repeatedly describes the ritual more graphically, directly, and tellingly: *dá menga pra Exu* (give blood to Exu).

It is midnight when the confirmations begin. The crowd that had come to consult with the old slaves is gone; only the personnel involved in the confirmations remain. Fernando takes his drum out back. The gate is locked. The usual handful of chickens and the big rooster who roam out back have been joined by more than a dozen hens and roosters brought for the occasion. Fernando pounds out a short coda, testing the sound. It sounds good. Seu Silva, or rather Tranca Rua, and Jorge make their way out back. Jorge calls back inside to the barracão: *"Elena, vem cá!"* (Elena, come here!). Jorge takes Elena by the shoulders and moves her to the center of the slab, a few feet in front of Tranca Rua. He brings her a young rooster, which she holds in one hand by the feet. Fernando starts to play, and we all sing, in a slow, minor key:

Exu, tem duas cabeças	Exu has two heads (faces)
Mas ele olha a sua banda com fé	But he looks over his band with faith
Uma é, satanás do inferno;	One (face) is that of Satan, from Hell
A outrá é,	The other is
De Jesus Nazaré	(that) of Jesus of Nazareth

Elena starts to shiver, though not from the cool night air. Her exu (called Marabô) is coming. Back and forth goes the tug of war of consciousness—Elena, Marabô, Elena, Marabô, Elena; the drumming, the song, the night, Tranca Rua right in front of her, the balance is tipping. Jorge takes the rooster and hands it to Tranca Rua. Tranca Rua touches it to Elena's head—a head now divided between Elena and Marabô—runs the rooster up and down her body front and back—just like a passe—and holds it up to the night. He cuts the head off, and the blood spurting from the jerking neck splatters on Elena's head and Elena-Marabô throws back his head and lets out an enormous belly laugh. Jorge hands Elena-Marabô a pack of cigarettes. Marabô takes out four and lights them all, smoking them in one big bunch as he cackles and jokes with us and enjoys himself immensely. Marabô and Elena are good for another year.

AXÉ

Axé is the force, the potential, the drive, the ceaseless energy of becoming. Axé is the power of the orixás. Axé is realized in living beings, crystallized in the sacred objects buried beneath the dirt floor of the House of Father John, fixed and made available in sacred plants and sacrificial blood and breath shaped into sacred speech. The Western dualism of spiritual and material is fundamental to the Umbanda cosmology—White or Afro-Brazilian—but axé, though pure spirit, pulses through life and vibrates through matter.

White Umbanda does not much use the word axé, and then usually in the plural, to refer to the sacred objects buried beneath the floor that are the "foundation" of a center. "Forces of nature," "vibrations," "energy" are the metaphors of choice, and, indeed, those are commonly used in Afro-Brazilian Umbanda discourse as well. At the House of Saint Benedict, that temple of White Umbanda, the metaphors of energy and vibrations construct an ethereal, disembodied, rarified force. But in Afro-Brazilian Umbanda, axé runs hot, like the blood that energizes Marabô for another year. At the House of Father John, axés are buried under the floor, but axés are also the flesh and blood of sacrifice—axés, plural, are the vessels of axé. And axé—its flows, its replenishment—is the unspoken theme of the bloody week of Tranca Rua.

THE BULL

The bull stood calmly, chewing his cud, gazing blankly at the handful of people doing—what? Surely nothing he had ever seen before in his couple of years in the country somewhere north of Rio. Nilsa, squatting on her heels, arranged new flowers at the base of the center post that connects earth and sky, past and future, while Mariana, Hilda, and Paulo touched base, conversing in soft but emphatic tones, eyes glistening with attention to each other's words. Fernando the drummer was way in the back where the audience sits, on the very last bench, wolfing down a plate of stewed chicken, rice and black beans, and manioc flour; I could feel his soul-deep satisfaction in that food more clearly than I could see him, which was clear indeed. For Fernando, with the ravenous appetite that comes with being twenty or a year or two more, extraordinarily vital and energetic, and poor, to have known hunger for days on end as a child and to fear it even now—that plate was heaped with axé, with life, with rightness in body and spirit, though Fernando would never say that. That is what I saw when I came in around eleven that night and passed by the bull in the darkness out back and followed his gaze into the barracão. My presence was starting to register on the bull, standing as I was several feet beyond the end of the rope tethering him to the tree. He tossed his head and pawed the ground. I proceeded inside.

Several of the men of the terreiro—I helped—had brought that bull down and tethered it the night before. A perfect specimen—it had to be, as Eduardo put it, without blemish, just like in the Bible—the black bull was the third of seven donated annually by a man who credited Tranca Rua with saving the life of his young son, diagnosed with a terminal illness. Though still a young bull, not yet grown immense, it was a real chore bringing him down the narrow steep path. Feet and head securely trussed, laying in the back of a flatbed truck on a canvas tarp, we slid it down some planks onto a big sheet of plywood, which theoretically would work as a kind of sled. It did, but not very well. Its real contribution was to protect the bull's hide as we pulled and lifted and pushed and slid the bull with all our might. I was soaked and spent by the time we got it out back and just watched as the two ranch hands who brought the bull rigged some ropes, securing the bull to a tree and an outbuilding. One of the men, a wiry, scarred, daredevil-looking man then slipped the knots immobilizing the deadly hooves and horns—and jumped straight up like a cat atop a low wall, narrowly avoiding first the kick and then the leaping charge of the animal. The bull lunged against the ropes several times, stood still, bucked, lunged, bucked some more. "*Caramba como é bravo*" (Damn, he's a wild one!), Eduardo said quietly. I detected admiration mixed with trepidation.

That was last night. Tonight the bull is quiet. He has been eating and resting. I walked into the dressing room. Eduardo was there with a couple of men who work in a slaughterhouse or a butcher shop—I never quite got

that straight. They had brought by several knives, professional butcher's
tools, wrapped in a blue towel. They would be back to pick them up early
in the morning. One of the men held up a dagger, and tapped his index
finger lightly on its point. Eduardo, a sturdy young man and spirited—
usually either joking or expressing his opinions emphatically or buzzing
around greeting everyone—looked really serious. I left him to himself.

Midnight came. Fernando took his drum out back where the bull
was, and we all joined him. Jorge cut the lights; moon and candles lit
the scene. Seu Silva, shirtless, in black pants with a red sash, sweated and
breathed heavily, his eyes far off. He was Tranca Rua. The mood was heavy,
heavy. Orlando and Zé were on top of the wall the man had jumped last
night. Somehow they brought the bull to the tree and tethered its head
securely against the trunk, high enough up so that its neck was stretched
and its front legs were fast against the wall. The bull bucked and kicked
with its back legs, but soon calmed as Fernando played very soft and slow;
I remember being absolutely sure, though having no way to know, that
Fernando's drum controlled the bull, just like it controlled the comings
and goings of spirits during sessions. I looked at Seu Silva/Tranca Rua.
Tears ran down his face.

It was time. From out at the gate I heard the shouted greeting of
Eduardo's cowboy spirit—"eeeeeyyup!" Moments later Boiadeiro (Cowboy,
as they called him, in place of a name) came around the corner, walking
in his bowlegged cowboy swagger. He walked by us but we were not in
his gaze. Fernando continued to play, softly, slowly, so deep. Eduardo/
Boiadeiro clomped up to the bull from behind, over its right shoulder. A
sudden flash of fire lit in the bull's eye; I knew it would buck and kick. It
didn't. Boiadeiro put his left hand up where the neck becomes the head,
kneading around with his fingers. Another flash in the bull's eye, and then
a steady, intense gleam. Boiadeiro reached into his sash and pulled out the
dagger the man had shown us earlier. Holding the dagger firmly in his
right hand and the point at the tip of the middle finger of his left hand,
he then placed his left hand over the daggered fist and drove the blade

through that narrow vulnerable place where the spinal cord meets the base of the brain. The light of the bull's eyes went out and the departing breath snorted out of the bull as he sagged dead against the ropes. The moment was electric. Like the burst of energy when a star collapses, axé burst forth as the life it animated extinguished.

The rest was mostly hard, bloody work. The body was laid out on a tarp. A big clay jar full of blood was drained from the neck, a little poured into a black bowl. Tranca Rua sweetened it with honey, and everyone took a sip. Working efficiently with the very good knives, Orlando and Zé butchered the bull. The head was cut off. Tranca Rua clutched it to his chest, weeping, overwhelmed. The genitals, liver, heart, and the feet were cut out and placed in a big clay bowl, along with the head and some blood. Those were the axés: the blood of life, the heart that pumps it and the liver that feeds it, the genitals that pass life on and drive living things forward, the feet that turn life-force into movement, and the head that directs and mediates force with consciousness. And then it was just mundane butchering, the conversion of dead life to conventional cuts of life-giving flesh food.

When the House of Father John reopened that Saturday with an all night, public celebration of Tranca Rua, the black hide of the bull was stretched on the wall. The clay bowl with the axés was arranged, surrounded by candles and bottles of cachaça and scotch, on an altar with Tranca Rua's cape as a backdrop. Tranca Rua glowed. His house was full, full of people, full of axé. It was a joyous night. The mournful song at the beginning of the week asked how much blood has been spilled on this cold ground; the celebration at the end seemed to ask a different question: how much life, how much spirit, how much axé has been danced and drummed and feasted up from this hot and fertile earth?

CHAPTER 8

The Mermaid's Song

Minha mãe é sereia . . .	My mother is a mermaid . . .
. . . com seu arpão na mão	. . . with her harpoon in hand
com seu canto da sereia	with her mermaid's song
ela vem aqui a terra trabalhar	she comes here to the earth to work

As I write these words, it has been twenty-two years and a couple of months since I first heard the mermaid's song. I could say that I heard it by chance; my plan had been to spend a few days in Rio de Janeiro and then fly up to Salvador to immerse myself in the traditional and storied Candomblé of Bahia. And then a friend of a friend and colleague took me to an Umbanda session at the little apartment of her aunt, Dona Luciana. Sitting in the living room I listened as her nephew Ronaldo and a woman sang a song calling on the cabocla Jurema, who comes from the snow, who comes from the sea, harpoon in hand, bringing the sacred leaves and the powers of Iemanjá, goddess of the sea. It was just then, from behind the half-opened door to the bedroom where Dona Luciana and Ronaldo and the singer stood before an altar stacked with images of Jesus, Santa Barbara, Our Lady of the Conception, Santa Anna, and saints George, Jerome, and Anthony, that the mermaid's song, soft at first as if shrouded in mist, then gathering force, rising and falling through octaves, clear, sweet, sad, haunting, alluring, impossibly strong, sailed forth, enveloping us all before falling away to disappear again into the mists of memory. I could say that I heard it by chance, but an Umbandista would say it was the orixás, not chance, not a friend of a friend, not me with my supposed free will, who brought me there that night, to hear the mermaid's song, a song to entice me to and guide me along my true path. In any event, I did not leave Rio that next week, nor the next month or the next, and I kept returning over the years to study Umbanda, which in the beginning I had emphatically chosen *not* to study (I was all about the Candomblé; Umbanda, from what I had read, was somehow less than authentic, made-up, a hodgepodge, gaudy, and kitsch). I would hear the mermaid's song many, many times over the years, and every time the goose bumps came, and they come even now when I listen to a tape I made of it, and, even more, they come when I listen to it in my memory.

There are not many ways to end a book. The one I resist most is to give conclusions, for two main reasons. First, conclusions, as they are usually written, treat the subject as an object, dead, finished, immobile, something about which we can make general, summary statements, as if to say: here in this book I have captured Umbanda, taken its measurements, revealed its structure, documented its history, and here I will put that all in a nutshell. But Umbanda for me is multiple (White Umbanda, Afro-Brazilian Umbanda, the House of Father John, the House of Saint Benedict, no Umbanda, just Umbandas) and, equally important, it is alive, moving, slippery, unfinished, emergent in the practices of Dona Luciana, Seu Silva, Ronaldo, Zé, and Cici, and countless thousands of others. That is what I have tried to present in this book, and that kind of presentation, subject matter aside, defies summation. "Conclusion" implies the final word; I don't believe in the final word, on anything. Second, of course, as a matter of courtesy and respect for the reader: you are quite capable of drawing your own conclusions, and I would not intrude on that private process.

So, I would like to end not with conclusions but with some reflections on what, metaphorically speaking, are the mermaid's songs that drew, and continue to draw, me as a scholar and as a human being to Umbanda. Some of these reflections, by the way, might suggest reasons why Umbanda is so attractive and relevant to so many Brazilians. Others relate more to the business of doing anthropology.

On that very night that I first heard the mermaid sing, I took communion from a French priest, martyred in the Amazon, I was knighted by a Spanish crusader, I spoke with an ancient Greek mariner, and I made the acquaintance of a silver-throated Portuguese girl. Over the years I would come to know an African king broken by slavery, a laughing flamenca dancer with a broken heart, a cowboy who cracked a bullwhip as he sang the praises of the breaking day and the Virgin Mary, an old slave telling tales of Atlantis and interplanetary journeys, and a stern Indian who taught me ways to be strong and clean in a dirty world. Those are just a few of the many characters I met. Whether understood as spirits or as the imaginative creations of actors who truly enter, body and soul, into the characters they portray (or both; perhaps in special places, say, between the covers of a novel or within the confines of an Umbanda session, distinctions of real and imaginary make no sense), these figures, the stories they told me and the stories told to me about them, captivated me. Through their language, gestures, and expressions, they became to me persons, friends who not only cared for me but invited me to enter magical places I had left behind as a child. While I have stated in this book that people come to Umbanda mainly to get spiritual help with real world problems, certainly I am not alone in my fascination with these spirits/ characters. And, their belief that these are spirits notwithstanding, I have no doubt that for mediums these are, or are also, important vehicles for creative self-expression.

As an anthropologist, I am especially struck by the ways these spirits or characters so often reflect, comment upon, and are imbedded in Brazilian cultural history. Noble savages seemingly drawn from the pages of José de Alencar; an old slave, Grandmother Catherine, who manifests herself through the body and voices of Ronaldo, tells a life story parallel, in parts, to the story of the slave Isaura in Bernardo de Guimarães's novel.[1] This is not to suggest a kind of plagiarism, but rather that Umbanda enacts, is steeped in, the themes and personages of national folklore and culture. But as we saw with the old slaves or the renegade priest received by Seu Silva, these representations are not just about the past; they are symbolic elements for thinking and commenting on the present. And, as we saw with the little street kid Rogério, the character or spirit can come not from the folkloric past but from the grim realities of the present. All this is important to me as an anthropologist, but it must surely also be part of what makes Umbanda so relevant to so many Brazilians.

Before I had actually begun working with Umbanda, I had little sense of the striking range of styles and practices in Umbanda. As we have seen, the kind of Umbanda practiced at the House of Saint Benedict—White Umbanda—is very different from the Afro-Brazilian Umbanda of the House of Father John. As an anthropologist and a student of Brazilian culture and history, this drew me like a magnet to Umbanda. From an anthropological or sociological perspective, we can read a whole history of hegemony and resistance, conformity and contestation, in the myths of Father John planting his root, the tales of Atlantis and Zélio de Morais's caboclo of the Seven Crossroads, in the pounding drums and blood sacrifices of the House of Father John, and in the careful, restrained dance steps and ethereal atmosphere of the House of Saint Benedict. White versus Afro-Brazilian Umbanda is the axis of diversity on which I focus mainly, and I think it is the most important, but Umbanda varies in so many other ways as well, from place to place and time to time. (For example, Dona Luciana devotes considerable energy and time to cultivating the "Oriental Line" of spirits; none of the other groups I worked with paid them any mind at all. Even at the very Afro-Brazilian House of Father John, some Umbandistas incorporated such decidedly non-African elements as tarot cards, numerology, and power or healing crystals.) This diversity of ritual and belief in Umbanda in part helps us understand how it has drawn followers from all points on the socioeconomic and ethnic spectrum: not one big tent, but many different tents from which to choose.

Most people, as I have said, come to Umbanda for spiritual support and assistance with real-world problems. Until the end of the decade I spent off and on in the field, my problems were few and minor, so I had (up until a final, life-altering ritual I performed with Dona Luciana on the afternoon of New Year's Eve, 1995, during my own time of crisis[2]) little firsthand, personal experience with this aspect of Umbanda. But I heard numerous testimonials from participants grateful for what the spirits had done for them: illnesses healed, marriages saved, addictions overcome, depressions lifted, rages soothed, and so on. And from mediums I heard over and over how taking up the path of caridade, of charity, had proven to be the way out of crisis and the way toward tranquility and balance. It must work, I thought (and think); most Umbanda mediums struck me as whole, healthy, strong people, coping well with sometimes difficult life circumstances. Umbanda, of whatever flavor, creates a supportive community (though there are conflicts and schisms—think of Dona Luciana's troubles early in her career as a medium), opens avenues for self-expression and self-actualization, and provides models upon which to map one's afflictions and paths toward healing, in the way that the eminent anthropologist Claude Lévi-Strauss describes for both shamanic healing and psychotherapy.[3]

My research with Umbanda challenged my views on the methods and objectives of anthropology, while confirming for me the basic soundness of the enterprise. For a long time I thought that anthropology was about describing the structure and functioning of a particular culture or subculture. Indeed, I had read monographs with titles like "Argonauts of the Western Pacific," and "The Nuer," and studies comparing aspects of various cultures, such as "Sex and Temperament in Three Primitive Societies."[4] The assumption is that there is a singular entity called the Nuer or the Tikopia, and that it can be described in isolation. But there was no singular Umbanda, there were different Umbandas, and within a given Umbanda center, say the House of Father John, different people had different understandings of Umbanda, and, what is more, even the views of individual persons varied situationally. What I had once thought to be the goal of fieldwork—to produce a concise model of a "culture"—looks now to me to be a fiction, an abstraction, a hopeless oversimplification that does no justice to that rich profusion or confusion of what is really out there. I would have rejected that goal—and I do reject it as a goal—but I came to realize that it was a necessary step toward making sense of that pullulating reality. To use a linguistic analogy: My interest is to understand these different voices, not to write a grammar; but, to understand those voices, I must first master that grammar. That "grammar," much of which I sketch out in the first chapter, describing the various categories of spirits and basic categories and concepts like charity and reincarnation, is a means to an end, not an end in itself.

Although my graduate training had gone far in undermining my naïve notions of anthropology as an objective science, the field translated that intellectual skepticism to the gut level of experience. My "sample" consisted of those I happened to meet, those who happened to put up with me; what I saw and heard were the things that happened when I happened to be there (or there, or there), that happened to register in my mind as significant—a criterion that certainly changed as my knowledge and perspective changed over time. Not to mention my biases—political, personal, aesthetic. But here again, while recognizing the impossibility of "scientific" objectivity—just as a concise model of Umbanda is a pragmatically necessary fiction—I have tried to honor the ideal of objectivity, if only in the breach.

There was a time, again, when I thought that anthropology, as a social science, was about explanation, tracing out the chains of cause and effect. I still believe that in human behavior there are causes and there are effects, though I believe that in many instances those causes are numerous, some of them unknown and maybe unknowable, and, in any event, mediated through those complex, motive-saturated, meaning-seeking, ambivalent, calculating, irrational, emotional, whimsical, and dead serious objects we call people, who by the way are always caught up in swirling constellations of relationships with other equally complex human beings. In this book I have tried to tease out some of those causes—historical, ideological—whose effects we presumably see in the various aspects of Umbanda; along with those causes—personal, biographical, circumstantial—that impel people toward the various paths of Umbanda. But far more important to me has been the task of conveying something of the richness of Umbanda as lived experience, so that you, too, in some distant way, through far too many of my words, might hear the mermaid's song.

Notes

INTRODUCTION

1. Possession and trance are the subjects of an extensive literature and long and lively debates: debates about what trance is, its relationship to possession beliefs, and the correlations between possession trance and societal features; possession and trance as means of redress and protest by disempowered groups, especially women; whether possession and trance should be addressed as culturally specific or pan-human, biologically based cognitive phenomena; the relationship of music, especially drumming, to the induction of trance; and biological correlates of trance, especially relating to sex and nutrition, to name a few major areas of contention. These debates are critical to a global understanding of possession and trance, but lie beyond the local, ethnographic scope of this book, where I am concerned not with what trance and possession are, but what the people I study do, and mean, through it. Among the sources an interested reader might consult regarding these important issues that I do not address are Janice P. Boddy (1989), Erika Bourguignon (1973, 1976), Emma Cohen (2007), Jean Comaroff (1985), Grace Harris (1957), Alice B. Kehoe (1983), Alice B. Kehoe and Dody H. Giletti (1981), Mary Keller (2002), Morton Klass (2003), Michael Lambek (1981), Ioan Lewis (1971), Raymond Prince (1966), and Gilbert Rouget (1985).

2. I discuss this history in Chapter 3 of this volume and the cosmology that came from it in Chapter 1.

3. Roger Bastide (1978) and Cândido Camargo (1961) link Umbanda to the emergence of the urban working class during the twentieth century. Diana Brown (1979, 1994) and Esther Pressel (1973, 1974), based on their ethnographic research during the 1960s in Rio de Janeiro and São Paulo, respectively, carry that analysis forward with insightful discussions placing the growth of Umbanda within the political contexts of that time and in the preceding decades. Patricia Lerch (1980) describes Umbanda in the southern city of Porto Alegre, while Chester E. Gabriel (1985) looks at Umbanda and other trance religions in the Amazonian city of Manaus. Seth and Ruth Leacock's 1975 ethnographic study of the Batuque in Belem (at the mouth of the Amazon) reveals both the interpenetration of Umbanda and Batuque and fascinating similarities and differences in practices and beliefs. In an ethnographically rich and analytically sophisticated book, John Burdick (1993) explores the dynamic relationship of Umbanda, liberation theology, and evangelical Protestantism within a working class community in Rio de Janeiro. I discuss representations of race,

slavery, and gender in a 1997 article; gender and identity in regard to the Afro-Brazilian deity Oxum (Hale 2001); ideology and identity in relation to Umbanda ritual aesthetics (2004); the historical development and contemporary shape of Umbanda (in press); and the deployment of symbolic substances in Umbanda ritual (in press). The journalist Alma Guillermoprieto gives an insightful, rich account of the shifting popularity of Umbanda in relation to evangelical Protestantism among the poor. Roberto da Matta (1981) employs Weberian categories and a structuralist approach to locate Umbanda within a national context of rituals and ethos. For those who read Portuguese, *Umbanda e Política*, edited by Diana Brown (1985), includes essays by Diana Brown, Maria Concone and Lísias Negrão, Patricia Birman, and Zélia Seiblitz that present detailed analyses of Umbanda's historical development and internal politics, and Umbanda's relationship with electoral politics during the period of military rule (1964–85). Renato Ortiz (1978) details the effects of racial and class prejudice in shaping Umbanda. Chester Gabriel (1985) describes the presence of Umbanda in the Amazonian city of Manaus. Peter Fry (1982) presents a comparative study of Umbanda in twentieth-century São Paulo and Methodism in nineteenth-century Manchester, England, in the context of rapid industrialization and urban growth.

4. Renato Rosaldo, in making the case for more vivid forms of ethnographic writing, makes the point better than I do: "much ethnography tells more about forms of activity in general than about how any particular instance was carried out. All too often in this process, lived experience is robbed of its vital significance" (1986: 103).

5. Michael Jackson (1989).

6. The program for this "interpretive anthropology" that views "culture as text" is laid out by Clifford Geertz in his essay "Thick Description: Towards an Interpretive Theory of Culture" (Geertz 1973).

7. Durkheim's contributions are many, but perhaps most important is his insistence that in social science such nonmaterial phenomena as values, beliefs, concepts, classificatory schemes, and other "collective representations" must be treated as things, as movers and shapers, in the same way that physical sciences deal with matter and energy. Durkheim's concept of the social fact as well as his views on what constitutes proper sociology (or social anthropology) is laid out in *The Rules of Sociological Method* (1964).

8. Geertz's essay "Religion as a Cultural System," can be found in his 1973 book *The Interpretation of Cultures*.

9. William James (1961).

10. Paul Stoller (1989) makes the case for an anthropology that takes the senses—the sights, smells, sounds, tastes, and tactility—seriously, as constitutive of lived experience. I attempt to do that.

11. See, for example, Max Weber (1993).

12. Out of respect for their privacy, names of people and places, along with certain identifying details, have been changed.

13. The Brazilian scholar Renato Ortiz (1978) documents the systematic suppression of practices that were thought to be "primitive," "barbaric"—code words, of course, for "African," in the development of what is referred to as "White Umbanda."

14. Physicists, for example, talk about the "observer effect," the idea that the mechanics of taking an observation affects the thing being observed—for example, a cloud chamber allows us to see the trajectory of a radioactive particle—but the media in the chamber necessarily alters the trajectory. An analogous example from my research: in Chapter 3 I allude to stories they tell at the House of Father John, about a root planted by an escaped slave, that constitute (and not just metaphorically) the foundation of their religious practice. Those stories were told at those moments because I was there and because I asked. No doubt the tellers took into account their assessments of my knowledge, linguistic abilities, attitudes, and so on. In effect, the telling of these stories—and the precise shapes the stories took—was inextricably tied to my presence as a listener.

15. My approach to writing ethnography and my understanding of what ethnographic research really is have been influenced by the fertile discussions of these issues over the last decades. To cite just a few of those influences, I would include Liza Abu-Lughod's 1991 essay, "Writing against Culture," the essays in James Clifford and George E. Marcus's *Writing Culture* (1986), Michael Jackson's *Paths Toward a Clearing* (1989), and Clifford Geertz's discussion of "experience near" versus "experience distant" perspectives in *Local Knowledge* (1983).

CHAPTER 1

*The title of this chapter alludes to Maria Laura Viveiros de Cavalcanti's 1983 book *O Mundo Invisível* (The Invisible World). Cavalcanti presents a clear, insightful, and detailed exposition of Spiritist cosmology and practice. Much of the Umbanda cosmology I describe in this chapter is adapted from Spiritism, and Cavalcanti's book helped me to ask the right questions and better understand what my friends were telling me.

1. Throughout this book, speech in quotations is as I remembered it and/or reported it in my notes, and translated so as to capture both the literal meaning and the style of the speaker, as I perceived it. I did some taping, but I found the presence of the tape recorder too distracting in conversations, so I largely restricted my use of the machine to recording music during rituals.

2. Roger Bastide (1978), Diana Brown (1994), and Esther Pressel (1973, 1974) offer useful discussions of Umbanda cosmology, as does (in Portuguese) Maria Concone (1987).

3. Such contributions are considered *caridade* (charity), a central virtue in Umbanda. While charity can take material form, as in this case, it also includes working with

the spirits (and, for spirits, working with Umbanda). Charity is valued in its own right, and it also contributes to one's karma and/or spiritual development.

4. Guaraná is a popular Brazilian soft drink made from the caffeine-rich seeds of the indigenous guaraná bush.

5. The term "exu" denotes a class of spirits, as described in this section, but it also refers to the intermediary between human beings and the orixás, whose proper name is Exu. In this book, I capitalize the intermediary.

6. When I first met Dona Luciana—twenty-one years before I wrote these words—I might have passed for a young man, at least to a much older person. Those days are long gone.

7. Xangô's sacrificial animal is the sheep—not the goat. Goats are not particularly associated with Xangô—this case, apparently, being an exception.

CHAPTER 2

1. While there is a tremendous diffusion of information regarding beliefs, doctrines, rituals, and so forth in books, pamphlets, and, increasingly, on the Internet, there is much secrecy in Afro-Brazilian religions, including Umbanda. In a fascinating and theoretically very sophisticated account of his work with a Candomblé terreiro in Rio, Paul Christopher Johnson (2002) documents how possession of secret knowledge marks position within the hierarchy while at the same time constituting the source of spiritual power and authenticity. Looking back, I can see that it would have been wiser to have seen the hypersecrecy I encountered with this group as not only understandable (though frustrating) but as a phenomenon worthy of patient and sympathetic study on my part. Live and learn. I should point out that although Dona Luciana, the House of Father John, and the House of Saint Benedict were far less secretive and, indeed, incredibly generous, there too I encountered secrets that would remain such.

2. "Macumba" is sometimes used to refer to Umbanda (though this is often taken as a pejorative term), and Umbanda, as we will see in the next chapter, has roots in the Macumba of the early decades of the twentieth century. For a fascinating theoretical analysis of Macumba as counterculture, see Marco Aurélio Luz and Georges Lapassade (1972).

3. Though written some decades earlier, the writing of journalist Paulo Barreto (who wrote under the name João do Rio) wonderfully conveys these attitudes and prejudices—while giving a great deal of useful, eyewitness information—in his fascinating 1905 (1976) book *As Religiões no Rio* (The Religions in Rio).

4. "Candomblé" is a generic term for Afro-Brazilian religions that are considered more traditional than Umbanda. Any given Candomblé terreiro will identify itself with a particular ancestral African "nation," such as Nagô (Yoruban), Gegê (Dahomean), or Angola. There is also Candomblé de Caboclo, which is less traditional in that it brings in indigenous American spirits and symbols. Candomblé is noted for highly

elaborated ritual, hierarchical social structure, lengthy initiations, and strong focus on the orixás as opposed to human spirits such as the pretos velhos, secrecy, and adherence to tradition. Despite the differences, Umbanda has its roots in Candomblé and exists in a kind of dialogue with it; any scholarly research on Umbanda requires a grounding in the literature of Candomblé. A very partial list of sources that have influenced my research would include Monique Augras (1983), José Flávio Barros (1993), Roger Bastide (1978, 1983), Edison Carneiro (1961, 1964, 1991), Beatriz Góis Dantas (1988), Mácio Goldman (1984), Paul Johnson (2002), Ruth Landes (1947), Vivaldo da Costa Lima (1977), James Lorand Matory (2005), Carlos Eugênio Marcondes de Moura (1981, 1982, 2000), Reginaldo Prandi (1991), René Ribeiro (1982), Juana Elbein dos Santos (1984), Pierre Verger (2002), Robert Voeks (1997), and Jim Wafer (1991).

5. "Seu" is derived from the word "Senhor" and, like Senhor, is used as a respectful form of address—similar to the way "Dona" is attached to the name of Luciana.

6. By "dance" he meant to suffer more of those episodes, to lose his mind, his health; to dance, helplessly, to the tune of insanity and suffering and death.

7. The first dissertation I read at the National Museum was that of Macio Goldman, an extraordinary study of the ritual construction of the person in Candomblé. As with numerous other theses and dissertations I read at the Museu Nacional, I benefited tremendously from both the content and the sophisticated analysis that marks the work of students of the graduate program in anthropology of the Federal University of Rio de Janeiro.

8. Yvonne Velho's book (1975) traces the history of an Umbanda terreiro from its beginning to its end—less than four months later—torn apart by brutal schismatic conflict. Victor Turner (1986) discusses (in English) the case, offering insights not only into the schism itself and the role of schism in Afro-Brazilian religion, but also an invaluable discussion of Umbanda in relation to the larger context of urban Brazil.

9. I of course wasn't there to witness this; my description is based on numerous observations, years later, of Dona Luciana when she received Jurema's spirit.

CHAPTER 3

1. The ritual lineage of *Omolocô*, according to Olga Guidolle Cacciatore's *Dicionário de Cultos Afro-Brasileiros*, "originates in the Angola nation, more particularly, perhaps, from the lunda-quico tribes. It stands out especially in Rio de Janeiro, linked to Umbanda" (1977: 193, translation mine).

2. Lévi-Strauss (1966) employs the metaphor of bricolage to elucidate the characteristics of mythical thinking. It seems to me an apt metaphor to apply to the active recombination of elements drawn from various sources that characterizes Umbanda.

3. To illustrate: in 1818, there were approximately 1,040,000 whites, 585,000 free Afro-Brazilians, and 1,930,000 Afro-Brazilian slaves, according to E. Bradford Burns

(1980: 147). Burns also reports that approximately two thirds of the population 1818 were either black or of partial African ancestry (55).

4. See Curtin 1969; Klein 1999: 211.

5. Burns 1980: 183.

6. Focusing on domestic servants in nineteenth-century Rio de Janeiro, Sandra Lauderdale Graham (1988) presents a fascinating social history of enslaved (and "free") women negotiating the urban environment. A. J. R. Russell-Wood (1982) gives a detailed overview of enslaved and free persons of African descent in the urban economy and society.

7. This is essentially the historical scenario that Roger Bastide presents in *The African Religions of Brazil* (1978).

8. Bastide gives an insightful survey of the diversity of slave origins, the main religious traditions, and the "syncretism and amalgamation" of these traditions with Catholicism in his *African Civilisations in the New World* (1971).

9. Bastide emphasizes the crucial importance of these brotherhoods in both *The African Religions of Brazil* (1978) and *African Civilisations in the New World* (1971).

10. Mané also goes by the name of Benedito, while another old slave spirit, at this same center, is called Mané as well. The two Manés are very different.

11. Mané on other occasions gave a much different, simpler account of how the Cabalans came to inhabit Earth. It seems that the Cabalans were pure spirit, but spirit, apparently, follows a version of the laws of physics. Over thousands of years, they grew so numerous that the planet's gravitational field couldn't hold them all. Some were spun off into space, wandering through the cosmos until they happened on planet Earth.

12. Paulo Berreto's book, *As Religiões no Rio*, was originally published in 1905.

13. The repression and stigmatization of Afro-Brazilian religion and the role of Afro-Brazilian religion in Bahian culture and daily life are central themes in Jorge Amado's *Tenda dos Milagres* (1969), available in English translation as *Tent of Miracles* (1971).

14. In her fascinating *Medo do Feitiço* (Fear of Sorcery) Yvonne Velho (1992) delves deeply into judicial and police records to document and analyze the repression of "sorcery" and Afro-Brazilian religious practices in turn of the century Rio de Janeiro.

15. Joaquim Manoel Macedo, *As Víctimas Algozes* (1869).

16. As an old slave spirit (preto velho) at the House of Father John, put it: "Let's say that you ask the velho to help you find a job. He does. All for the good, right? Well, maybe your getting that job means someone else goes without work, maybe his family goes hungry." Several Umbandistas and their spirits made this argument to me, presenting various scenarios in which good for one means harm for another.

17. While I place this in quotation marks, this is not a verbatim report of the spirit's actual speech—rather, it is a construction based on what Cici reported the spirit had told her.

18. David J. Hess (1991: 17).

19. João do Rio also reports that Spiritism attracted "our most lucid minds," and that thousands of Spiritists could be found among the physicians, lawyers, the press, professors, and the military (Barreto 1976 [1905]: 154–56).

20. Israel Cysneiros (1983: 99–100), *Umbanda: Poder e Magia* (Umbanda: Power and Magic). My translation.

21. Brown (1994: 39).

22. See, for example, Ronaldo Linares (1988).

23. Brown (1994: 39–40).

CHAPTER 4

1. Eventually, Seu Alberto turned up. No one (except me) seemed very happy to see him, but no one displayed any hostility. He told me simply that he had been "traveling"—and that was all I got out of him.

2. John Burdick (1998) discusses the myth and media representations of Anastácia, her problematic position among black movement activists and the Catholic Church, and the ideological (and personal) significance of how she is perceived by black, white, and mixed race women.

3. As discussed in Paula Montero (1985).

4. *Sinha Moça* was an extremely popular miniseries or telenovela during my first visit to Brazil during June through August of 1986. *A Escrava Isaura* (Bernardo Guimarães [1988]) was originally published in 1875.

5. Bastide's *The African Religions of Brazil* (1978, originally published in French in 1960) continues to be a touchstone for any research on Afro-Brazilian religions.

6. In what is undoubtedly the most influential book in Brazilian literature, *Casa Grande e Senzala* (1992, available in English translation as *The Masters and the Slaves*), Gilberto Freyre presents a historical-anthropological argument celebrating a miscegenized Brazilian national identity. First published in 1933, Freyre's book powerfully repudiated the racist self-loathing that characterized most elite discourse about national and racial identity in Brazil. Interestingly enough, sexuality plays a central role in Freyre's historical anthropology, as it does in the narratives of many of the old slaves.

CHAPTER 5

1. Diana Brown, *Umbanda: Religion and Politics in Urban Brazil* (1994: 65).

2. Dozens of these books were available to me before I went to Brazil, in the Nettie Lee Benson Latin American Collection of the University of Texas at Austin libraries.

3. Diana Brown (1994), Roger Bastide (1978).

4. Brown (1994: 65).

5. "Ponto," literally "point," refers to the signature a spirit makes to establish his identity on arriving in an Umbanda center. The ponto is usually composed of indexical and iconic signs referring to the spirit's identity; a ponto for the caboclo Seven Arrows, for example, might contain a bow and seven arrows, while Jurema's ponto includes representations of waves. These are called "*pontos riscados*," literally, "drawn points"; the songs that call spirits are "*pontos cantados*" (sung points). In the pontos cantados, language is used to both invoke and *evoke* the spirit.

6. Oxossi is an Orixá, or African deity. Oxossi, a hunter, is the patron of the forests. His implements are the bow and arrow, and he is often associated with caboclos.

7. Diana Brown (1994: 72) makes precisely this point.

8. Edison Carneiro (1964: 143–51) cites numerous instances where caboclo names and place names are drawn from the nineteenth-century Indianist literature, especially from José de Alencar (a point taken up in Brown 1994: 65–67), but he also argues that precedents for caboclo-type figures are to be found among the peoples of Angola and Congo, pre-dating the influence of Indianist literature. He points out, for example, that pontos cantados frequently state that caboclos come from Aruanda, which he identifies with Luanda (a port in Angola from which hundreds of thousands of slaves were shipped to Brazil). But as Diana Brown points out, correctly in my view, for many Umbandistas, Aruanda is a place in the astral—not a reference to Africa (1994: 67).

9. Though Dona Luciana used the word "banco" (bank), I assume she really meant "casa de penhores" (pawn shop), however, I chose to retain her own usage here.

CHAPTER 6

1. Olga Guidolle Cacciatore (1977: 197).

2. In his beautiful book *Mitologia dos Orixás* (2005), Reginaldo Prandi presents three hundred stories about the various orixás. The late Pierre Verger, a Candomblé initiate, photographer, and scholar of African and Afro–New World religion, presents a well-researched discussion about orixás (along with striking photographs) in his *Orixás, Deuses Iorubás na África e no Novo Mundo* (1981).

3. Usually, the orixá da frente is of the same sex as the person, while the second is opposite. But sometimes these are reversed, or both the orixá de frente and the

second may be of the same sex, either the same or opposite of the individual in question. A reversal can result in one being gay or lesbian, while having both orixás of the same sex can result in hypermasculinity or hyperfemininity. See Birman (1988) for an interesting discussion.

4. Augras (1983) presents a detailed and sophisticated analysis of the orixás as signs of and models for personal identity. Also, see Augras 1991; additional insights were gained through personal communication with Augras.

5. Cascudo (1954: 89).

6. For an insightful discussion of the syncretism controversy, as well as richly detailed exploration of the dynamic interplay of Candomblé, Catholicism, evangelical Protestantism, and politics, see Selka (2007).

7. My perspective on metaphor is informed by James W. Fernandez's clear and insightful discussion in *Persuasions and Performances: The Play of Tropes in Culture* (1986).

8. I observed two exceptions at Dona Luciana's: one night Ogum incorporated in Ronaldo to show me the beads I would wear as a son of Ogum; on another night, Omolu, unbidden, possessed Ronaldo.

9. Jim Wafer (1991: 86).

10. Reginaldo Prandi (2001: 152–61). Pierre Verger, the French ethnologist who spent much of his ninety-three years as a Candomblé initiate, also uses the masculine forms and (like Prandi) makes no mention of Ossaim's alleged bisexuality in his study of orixás in Africa and the New World (Verger [1981: 122–24]).

11. I quote Macedo (1869) earlier, in Chapter 3 of this volume.

12. Wafer (1991: 174).

13. This is not the same as "going native." Rather, it is more like what one does in reading a novel or watching a film or a play: a suspension of disbelief, an active engagement with the assumptions and world view of the artist, in short, to enter into the spirit of the thing, until the final page or the closing curtain. But like a great novel or film, the book never really closes and the curtain never truly comes down: Umbanda has left deep marks on my consciousness and my soul.

14. This and the next story about Ogum can be found in Prandi (2005).

CHAPTER 7

*The title alludes to an essay written by Delores J. Shapiro, "Blood, Oil, Honey, and Water: Symbolism in Spirit Possession Sects in Northeastern Brazil" (1995). Shapiro's essay explores how in these various sects (Candomblé, Giro, and Mesa Branca), blood, honey, oil, and water constitute metaphors of racial identity and ideology, in much the same way that blood and water work within and between Afro-Brazilian and White Umbanda.

1. After reading Bakhtin's book about Rabelais, I felt at times as though I could hear in his discussion of medieval laughter echoes of the rollicking cackles of some of the exus and pomba-giras I have known.

2. Arruda (Ruta graveolens) is known as Rue in English. Guiné (Petivena alliacea) is called Anamu in Guinea and Henweed in English.

CHAPTER 8

1. Guimarães (1998 [1875]).

2. See Hale (2009a).

3. Lévi-Strauss (1963).

4. Bronislaw Malinowski (1961 [1922]); E. E. Evans-Pritchard (1969 [1940]); and Margaret Mead (1935), respectively.

Glossary

azeite de dendê: A reddish orange oil derived from the dendê palm.

barracão: Literally a large tent, "barracão" is often used to refer to the main building of an Umbanda center where public rituals are held.

boiadeiro: The spirit of a cowboy from the semiarid, often drought-stricken Northeast. Boiadeiros are typically classified as a kind of caboclo.

caboclo: The spirit of a Brazilian Indian. Outside of the context of Umbanda and Afro-Brazilian religion, the word refers to acculturated Indians and peasants of indigenous and mixed heritage of the northeastern backlands.

Candomblé: A generic term for Afro-Brazilian religion thought to be more "traditional" than Umbanda. There are various "nations" of Candomblé, such as Angola and Nagô, that trace their ritual to different locales in Africa. Generally speaking, Candomblé ritual is focused on the orixás, while Umbanda is more involved with human spirits such as caboclos and pretos velhos.

caridade: Literally "charity," this usually refers to the work that spirits and mediums do for those who come to consult with them. The spirit performs charity by giving advice and ritual treatments, such as passes; the medium performs charity by serving as the vehicle for the spirit. Both, in turn, improve their karma.

Carioca: Native of or to Rio de Janeiro

criança: A child-spirit

centro: Literally "center," a place where Umbanda is practiced.

exu: In Umbanda, "exu" generally refers to a "less evolved" spirit; these are often colorful characters—carousers, bohemians, petty criminals, and so on. Despite their low status, they are highly valued as advisors and allies. In Candomblé, an Exu is the intermediary between human beings and orixás. In both Umbanda and Candomblé, exus are considered indispensable.

exus da luz or exus batizados: Literally "exus of the light" and "baptized exus," respectively, these are exus that have seen the error of their ways and seek to make amends and improve their karma by working through Umbanda mediums.

exus das trevas: "exus of the shadows," these are unredeemed exus who work for evil, either directly or through feiticeiros and/or practitioners of Quimbanda.

favela: Generally translated as "shantytown," a favela is a community of working-class and lower-income people. Dwellings in a favela are generally built by their occupants, often over a period of many years as they acquire building materials. Sewage, water, and electrical services also are usually improvised by residents. Titles to land and homes are often nonexistent or irregular. Favelas have a reputation for violence and crime, most of which in recent years is associated with the drug trade, but favelas are also marked by a strong sense of community and cultural vibrancy. Many favelas are perched on steep mountainsides abutting some of the wealthiest neighborhoods. There are approximately three hundred favelas in Rio de Janeiro, housing approximately a quarter of the population.

feiticeiro: One who practices sorcery or black magic; some of the caridade of Umbanda consists of counteracting the work of feiticeiros.

Jurema: Variously, the name of a female cobocla spirit, a species of tree (pithecolobium torta, an acacia-like tree also known as mimosa), and a psychotropic tea brewed from its leaves.

karma: The idea, very prevalent in Umbanda, that good and bad acts affect the spiritual evolution and future condition of the individual, while one's present level of spiritual evolution and life circumstances are, in part at least, a result of actions in previous incarnations.

mãe de santo: Literally "mother of saint"; a woman who acts as the spiritual and temporal leader in an Afro-Brazilian terreiro or centro.

obsessor (or espírito obsessor): An unevolved spirit who, whether out of malevolence or not, attacks and/or possesses its living victims, causing illnesses, delusions, anxieties, rages, and other symptoms. Good spirits, performing caridade through Umbanda mediums, occasionally detect and expel these spirits during their consultations.

orixá: Variously (and often simultaneously) conceived of as an African deity, a force of nature, a vibration, and a spiritual quality.

pai de santo: Literally "father of saint"; a man who acts as the spiritual and temporal leader in an Afro-Brazilian terreiro or centro.

passe: A ritual performed by a spiritual entity incorporated in a medium, which consists of running the hands up and down the length of the body, front and back, of the person receiving the passe, usually without actually touching. The passe transmits positive energies while removing negative energies and impurities.

pomba-gira: Female equivalent of exu in Umbanda

ponto cantado: A hymn or song used to summon, celebrate, or send away a spiritual entity, or to mark or provide meta-commentary on particular parts of a ritual.

ponto riscado: A design, drawn by a medium incorporating a spirit, that serves as a signature of the spirit and may in itself be imbued with spiritual force. Design elements include references to various spiritual traditions (e.g., the Star of David, the Cross, the Yin-Yang symbol), geographical and astronomical features (such as waves, constellations, crescent and full moons), and cultural traits of the spirit (the ponto riscado for a caboclo might include a brace of arrows, a bow, or a tomahawk).

preto velho: Literally "old black," the spirit of an old Afro-Brazilian slave. The feminine is preta velha.

Quimbanda: A kind of inverted, evil twin of Umbanda that deals with evil spirits and evil forces.

Rocinha: The largest favela in Rio de Janeiro, Rocinha is perched on a mountainside abutting two of Rio's wealthiest South Zone neighborhoods, and overlooking the ocean. Rocinha is more developed than most favelas, with bus service, banks, pharmacies, and other formal sector businesses. Population estimates range from sixty thousand to three hundred thousand or more.

tenda: Literally "tent," a place where Umbanda is practiced. The word is often used in conjunction with the name of the guiding spirit of the leader of an Umbanda group as the proper name of the place of worship, for example, a Tenda de Tupinambá (the Tent of Tupinambá).

terreiro: A building or group of buildings where Afro-Brazilian religion is practiced. The word also means "a clearing," a reference to the outdoor celebration of Afro-Brazilian religion during slavery.

toque: A drum rhythm or assemblage of rhythms used to summon, celebrate, or send away a spiritual entity, or to mark particular moments of ritual.

References

Abu-Lughod, Lila

    1991   "Writing Against Culture." In *Recapturing Anthropology: Working in the Present*, edited by Richard G. Fox, 137–62. Santa Fe: School of American Research Press.

Amado, Jorge

    1969   *Tenda dos Milagres*. São Paulo: Martins.

    1971   *Tent of Miracles*. New York: Knopf.

Augras, Monique

    1983   *O Duplo e a Metamorfose*. Petropolis, Brazil: Editora Vozes, Ltda.

Bakhtin, Mikhail Mikhailovich

    1968   *Rabelais and His World*. Cambridge, MA: MIT Press.

Barreto, Paulo (João do Rio)

    1976   [1905] *As Religiões no Rio*. Rio de Janeiro: Novo Aguilar.

Barros, José Flávio Pessoa de

    1993   *O Segredo das Folhas: Sistema de Classificação de Vegetais no Candomblé Jeje-Nagô do Brasil*. Rio de Janeiro: Pallas.

Bastide, Roger

    1971   *African Civilisations in the New World*. New York: Harper & Row.

    1978   *he African Religions of Brazil*. Baltimore: John Hopkins University Press.

    1983   *Estudos Afro-Brasileiros*. São Paulo: Editora Perspectiva.

Birman, Patricia

    1980   "Feitiço, Carrego, e Olho Grande; Os Males do Brasil São: Estudo de um Centro de Umbanda numa Favela do Rio de Janeiro." Unpublished Master's thesis, Universade Federal do Rio de Janeiro/Museo Nacional.

    1985   "Registrado em Cartório, com Firma Reconhecida: a Mediação Política das Federações da Umbanda." In *Umbanda e Política*, edited by Diana Brown, editor, 80–121. Rio de Janeiro: Editora Marco Zero.

1988 "Fazer Estilo Criando Gêneros." Unpublished PhD Dissertation, Universade Federal do Rio de Janeiro/Museo Nacional.

Boddy, Janice P.

1989 *Wombs and Alien Spirits: Women, Men, and the Zar cult in Northern Sudan.* Madison: University of Wisconsin Press.

Bourguignon, Erika

1973 *Religion, Altered States of Consciousness, and Social Change.* Columbus: Ohio State University Press.

1976 *Possession.* San Francisco: Chandler and Sharp Publishers.

Brown, Diana

1979 "Umbanda and Class Relations in Brazil." In *Brazil, Anthropological Perspectives,* edited by Maxine Margolis and William Carter, 270–305. New York: Columbia University Press.

1985 "Uma Hisotória da Umbanda no Rio." In *Umbanda e Política,* edited by Diana Brown, 9–42. Rio de Janeiro: Editora Marco Zero.

1994 *Umbanda: Religion and Politics in Urban Brazil.* New York: Columbia University Press.

Burdick, John

1993 *Looking for God in Brazil: The Progressive Catholic Church in Urban Brazil's Religious Arena.* Berkeley: University of California Press.

1998 *Blessed Anastácia: Women, Race, and Popular Christianity in Brazil.* New York: Routledge.

Burns, E. Bradford

1980 *A History of Brazil.* 2nd ed. New York: Columbia University Press.

Cacciatore, Olga Guidolle

1977 *Dicionário de Cultos Afro-Brasileiros.* Rio de Janeiro: Forense Universitária.

Camargo, Cândido Procôpio Ferreira de

1961 *Kardecismo e Umbanda.* São Paulo: Livraria Pioneira Editora.

Carneiro, Edison

1961 *Candomblés da Bahia.* Rio de Janeiro: Conquista.

1964 *Ladinos e Crioulos: Estudos sobre o Negro no Brasil.* Rio de Janeiro: Editôra Civilização Brasileira.

1991 *Religiões Negras; Negros Bantos.* Rio de Janeiro: Civilização Brasileira.

Cascudo, Câmara

　1954　*Dicionário de Folclore Brasileiro*. Rio de Janeiro: Brasileira de Ouro.

Cavalcanti, Maria Laura Viveiros de Castro

　1983　*O Mundo Invisível: Cosmologia, Sistema Ritual e Noção de Pessoa no Espíritismo*. Rio de Janeiro: Zahar Editores.

Clifford, James, and George E. Marcus, eds.

　1986　*Writing Culture: The Poetics and Politics of Ethnography*. Berkeley: University of California Press.

Cohen, Emma

　2007　*The Mind Possessed: The Cognition of Spirit Possession in an Afro-Brazilian Religious Tradition*. Oxford: Oxford University Press.

Comaroff, Jean

　1985　*Body of Power, Spirit of Resistance: The Culture and History of a South African People*. Chicago: University of Chicago Press.

Concone, Maria Helena Vilas Boas

　1987　*Umbanda, uma Religiao Brasileira*. Sao Paulo: FFLCH/USP-CER.

Concone, Maria Helena Vilas Boas, and Lísias Nogueira Negrão

　1985　"Umbanda: da Representação á Cooptacão. O Envolvimento Político Partidario da Umbanda Paulista nas Eleições de 1982." In *Umbanda e Política*, edited by Diana Brown, 43–79. Rio de Janeiro: Editora Marco Zero.

Curtin, Phillip D.

　1969　*The Atlantic Slave Trade: A Census*. Madison: University of Wisconsin Press.

Cysneiros (Omolubá)

　1983　*Umbanda: Poder e Magia*. Rio de Janeiro: Sindicato Nacional dos Editôres de Livros.

Dantas, Beatriz Góis

　1988　*Vovó Nagô e Papai Branco: Uso e Abusos de África no Brasil*. Rio de Janeiro: Graal.

Durkheim, Emile

　1964　*The Rules of Sociological Method*. Edited by George E. B. Catlin; translated by Sarah A Solovay and John H. Mueller. New York: Free Press of Glencoe.

Eliade, Mircea

　1972　*Shamanism: Archaic Techniques of Ecstasy*. Princeton: Princeton University Press.

Evans-Pritchard, E. E.

    1969   *The Nuer: A Description of the Modes of Livelihood and Political Institutions of a Nilotic People*. New York: Oxford University Press.

Fernandez, James W.

    1986   *Persuasions and Performances: The Play of Tropes in Culture*. Bloomington: Indiana University Press.

Foster, George

    1965   "Peasant Society and the Image of Limited Good." *American Anthropologist* 67(2): 293–315.

Freyre, Gilberto

    1992   [1933] *Casa Grande e Senzala: Formação da Família Brasileira sob o Regime da Economia Patriarcal*. Rio de Janeiro: Record.

Fry, Peter

    1982   *Para Inglês Ver: Identidade e Política na Cultura Brasileira*. Rio de Janeiro: Zahar Editores.

Gabriel, Chester E.

    1985   *Comunicações dos Espíritos: Umbanda, Cultos Regionais em Manaus e a Dinâmica do Transe Mediúnico*. São Paulo: Edições Loyola.

Geertz, Clifford

    1973   "Thick Description: Toward an Interpretive Theory of Culture" and "Religion as a Cultural System." In *The Interpretation of Cultures: Selected Essays*, 3–32 and 87–125. New York: Basic Books.

    1983   *Local Knowledge: Further Essays in Interpretive Anthropology*. New York: Basic Books.

Goldman, Mácio

    1984   "A Possessão e a Construção Ritual da Pessoa no Candomblé." Unpublished Master's thesis, Universade Federal do Rio de Janeiro/Museo Nacional.

Graham, Sandra Lauderdale

    1988   *House and Street: The Domestic World of Servants and Masters in Nineteenth-Century Rio de Janeiro*. Austin: University of Texas Press.

Guillermoprieto, Alma

    1994   *The Heart the Bleeds: Latin America Now*. New York: Vintage Books.

Guimarães, Bernardo de

    1988   *A Escrava Isaura*. São Paulo: Editora Ática.

Hale, Lindsay

1997   "Preto Velho: Resistance, Redemption, and En-Gendered Representations of
        Slavery in a Brazilian Possession-Trance Religion." *American Ethnologist* 24(2):
        392–414.

2001   "Mama Oxum: Reflections on Gender and Sexuality in Brazilian Umbanda."
        In *Osun Across the Waters: A Yoruba Goddess in Africa and the Americas*, edited
        by Joseph M. Murphy and Mei-Mei Sanford, 213–29. Bloomington: Indiana
        University Press.

2004   "The House of Saint Benedict, The House of Father John: Umbanda
        Aesthetics and a Politics of the Senses." In *Race, Nation, and Religion in the
        Americas*, edited by Henry Goldschmidt and Elizabeth McAlister, 283–304.
        Oxford: Oxford University Press.

2009a   "Umbanda." In *Religion and Society in Latin America: Interpretive Essays from
        the Conquest to the Present*, edited by Lee M. Penyak and Walter J. Petry, n.p.
        Maryknoll, NY: Orbis.

2009b   "Spiritual Matters: The Aesthetics of Ritual Substances in Umbanda." In *Black
        Religion and Aesthetics: Religious Life and Thought in Africa and the African
        Diaspora*, edited by Anthony Pinn, n.p. New York: Palgrave Macmillan.

Harris, Grace

1957   "Possession 'Hysteria' in a Kenya Tribe." *American Anthropologist* 59(6):
        1046–66.

Heidegger, Martin

1982   *The Basic Problems of Phenomenology*. Bloomington: Indiana University Press.

Hess, David J.

1991   *Spirits and Scientists: Ideology, Spiritism, and Brazilian Culture*. University
        Park: Pennsylvania State University Press.

Husserl, Edmund

1977   *Cartesian Meditations: An Introduction to Phenomenology*. The Hague: M.
        Nijhoff.

Jackson, Michael

1989   *Paths Toward a Clearing: Radical Empiricism and Ethnographic Inquiry*.
        Bloomington: Indiana University Press.

Johnson, Paul Christopher

2002   *Secrets, Gossip, and Gods: The Transformation of Brazilian Candomblé*. Oxford:
        Oxford University Press.

Kehoe, Alice B.

1983   "Reply to Lewis and Bourguignon, Bellisari and McCabe." *American
        Anthropologist* 85(2): 416–17.

Kehoe, Alice B., and Dody H. Geletti

    1981   "Women's Preponderance in Possession Cults: The Calcium Deficiency Hypothesis Extended." *American Anthropologist* 83(3): 549–61.

Keller, Mary

    2002   *The Hammer and the Flute: Women, Power, and Spirit-Possession.* Baltimore: Johns Hopkins University Press.

Klass, Morton

    2003   *Mind over Mind: The Anthropology and Psychology of Spirit Possession.* Lanham, MD: Rowman & Littlefield.

Klein, Herbert S.

    1999   *The Atlantic Slave Trade.* Cambridge: Cambridge University Press.

Lambek, Michael

    1981   *Human spirits: A Cultural Account of Trance in Mayotte.* Cambridge: Cambridge University Press.

Landes, Ruth

    1947   *The City of Women.* New York: Macmillan.

Leacock, Seth, and Ruth Leacock

    1975   *Spirits of the Deep: A Study of an Afro-Brazilian Cult.* Garden City, New York: Anchor Books.

Lerch, Patricia

    1980   "Spirit Mediums in Umbanda Evangelada of Porto Alegre, Brazil." In *A World of Women,* edited by Erika Bourguignon, 129–59. New York: Praeger.

Lévi-Strauss, Claude

    1963   "The Sorcerer and His Magic" and "The Effectiveness of Symbols." In *Structural Anthropology,* 165–85 and 186–205. New York: Basic Books.

    1966   *The Savage Mind.* Chicago: The University of Chicago Press.

Lewis, Ioan

    1971   *Ecstatic Religion: An Anthropological Study of Spirit Possession and Shamanism.* Harmondsworth, England: Penguin Books.

Lima, Vivaldo da Costa

    1977   *A Família do Santo nos Candomblés Jeje-Nagô da Bahia.* Salvador: Universidade Federal da Bahia.

Linares, Ronaldo António

1988   "Como Conheci Zélio de Morães, O Pai da Umbanda" and "Mais um
       Pouquinho Sobre Zélio de Morães." In *Iniciação à Umbanda*, vol. 2, edited
       by Diamatino Fernandes Trindade, 15–19 and 21–25. São Paulo: Icone Editora.

Luz, Marco Aurélio, and Georges Lapassade

1972   *O Segredo da Macumba*. Rio de Janeiro: Paz e Terra.

Macedo, Joaquim Manoel de

1869   *As Victimas Algozes*. Rio de Janeiro: Typ. American.

Malinowski, Bronislaw

1961   *Argonauts of the Western Pacific*. New York: E. P. Dutton.

Matory, James Lorand

2005   *Black Atlantic Religion: Tradition, Transnationalism, and Matriarchy in the
       Afro-Brazilian Candomblé*. Princeton: Princeton University Press.

Matta, Roberto da

1981   "The Ethic of Umbanda and the Spirit of Messianism: Reflections on the
       Brazilian Model." In *Authoritarian Capitalism: Brazil's Contemporary Economic
       and Political Development*, edited by Thomas C. Bruneau and Phillipe Faucher,
       239–63. Boulder, CO: Westview Press.

Mead, Margaret

1935   *Sex and Temperament in Three Primitive Societies*. New York: W. Morrow.

Merleau-Ponty, Maurice

1974   *Phenomenology, Language and Perception: Selected Essays of Maurice Merleau-
       Ponty*. London: Heinemann.

Montero, Paula

1985   *Da Doença á Desordem*. Rio de Janeiro: Graal.

Moura, Carlos Eugênio Marcondes de

1981   *Olòòrìsà: Escritos Sobre a Religião dos Orixás*. São Paulo: Agora.

1982   *Bandeira de Alairá: Outros Escritos Sobre a Religião dos Orixás*. São Paulo:
       Nobel.

2000   *Candomblé: Religião de Corpo e da Alma: Tipos Psicoloógicos nas Religiões
       Afro-Brasileiras*. Rio de Janeiro: Pallas.

Ortiz, Renato

1978   *A Morte Branca do Feiticeiro Negro*. Petropolis, Rio de Janeiro: Editora Vozes.

Prandi, Reginaldo

  1991   *Os Candomblés de São Paulo: A Velha Magia na Metrópole Nova.* São Paulo: Editora Huisitec.

  2005   *Mitologia dos Orixás.* São Paulo: Companhia das Letras.

Pressel, Esther J.

  1973   "Umbanda in São Paulo: Religious Innovation in a Developing Society." In *Religion, Altered States of Consciousness and Social Change,* edited by E. Bourguignon, 264–318. Columbus: Ohio State University Press.

  1974   "Umbanda: Trance and Possession in São Paulo." In *Trance, Healing, and Hallucination,* edited by F. Goodman, J. Henney, and E. Pressel, 113–225. New York: John Wiley & Sons.

Prince, Raymond

  1966   *Trance and Possession States.* Montreal: R. M. Bucke Memorial Society.

Ribeiro, René

  1982   *Antropologia da Religião e Outros Estudos.* Recife: Editora Massangana.

Rosaldo, Renato

  1986   "Ilongot Hunting as Story and Experience." In *The Anthropology of Experience,* edited by Victor W. Turner and Edward M. Bruner, 97–138. Urbana and Chicago: University of Illinois Press.

Rouget, Gilbert

  1985   *Music and Trance: A Theory of the Relations Between Music and Possession.* Chicago: University of Chicago Press.

Russell-Wood, A. J. R.

  1982   *The Black Man in Slavery and Freedom in Colonial Brazil.* London: Macmillan Press.

Sangirardi Jr.

  1988   *Deuses da África e do Brasil: Candomblé e Umbanda.* Rio de Janeiro: Editora Civilização Brasileira.

Santos, Juana Elbein dos

  1984   *Os Nagô e a Morte: Pàde, Asèsè e o Culto Ègun na Bahia.* Petropolis: Vozes.

Seiblitz, Zélia

  1985   "A gira Profana." In *Umbanda e Política,* edited by Diana Brown, 122–54. Rio de Janeiro: Editora Marco Zero.

Selka, Stephen

    2007   *Religion and the Politics of Ethnic identity in Bahia, Brazil.* Gainesville: University of Florida Press.

Shapiro, Dolores J.

    1995   "Blood, Oil, Honey, and Water: Symbolism in Spirit Possession Sects in Northeastern Brazil." *American Ethnologist* 22(4): 828–47.

Stoller, Paul

    1989   *The Taste of Ethnographic Things: The Senses in Anthropology.* Philadelphia: University of Pennsylvania Press.

Turner, Victor

    1986   "Social Dramas in Brazilian Umbanda: The Dialectics of Meaning." In *The Anthropology of Performance*, edited by Victor Turner, 33–71. New York: PAJ Publications.

Velho, Yvonne Maggie

    1975   *Guerra de Orixá: Um Estudo de Ritual e Conflito.* Rio de Janeiro: Zahar.

    1992   *Medo do Feitiço: Relações entre Magia e Poder no Brasil.* Rio de Janeiro: Arquivo Nacional, Orgao do Ministério da Justica.

Verger, Pierre Fatumbi

    1981   *Orixás, Deuses Iorubás na África e no Novo Mundo.* São Paulo: Corrupio.

    2002   *Saida da Iaô: Cinco Ensaios sobre a Religião dos Orixás.* São Paulo: Fundação Pierre Verger, Axis Mundi Editora.

Voeks, Robert A.

    1997   *Sacred Leaves of Candomblé: African Magic, Medicine, and Religion in Brazil.* Austin: University of Texas Press.

Wafer, Jim

    1991   *The Taste of Blood: Spirit Possession in Brazilian Candomblé.* Philadelphia: University of Pennsylvania Press.

Weber, Max

    1993   *The Sociology of Religion.* Boston: Beacon Press.

Index

CPSIA information can be obtained
at www.ICGtesting.com
Printed in the USA
LVHW110724090121
676114LV00030B/192